05/04
32

THE BOYS FROM LIVERPOOL
John,
Paul,
George,
Ringo

Nicholas Schaffner

THE BOYS FROM LIVERPOOL
John,
Paul,
George,
Ringo

METHUEN

NEW YORK

Library of Congress Cataloging in Publication Data

Schaffner, Nicholas
The boys from Liverpool.

Bibliography: p. 192
Includes index.
SUMMARY: Profiles the individual and collective careers
of the rock music group that made a phenomenal
impact on the popular music world in the 1960's.
1. Beatles—Juvenile literature.   2. Rock musicians—
England—Biography—Juvenile literature.
[1. Beatles.   2. Musicians.   3. Rock music] I. Title.
ML3930.B39S3   784'.092'2   [B] [920]   79-25917
ISBN 0-416-30661-6

Manufactured in the United States of America by
Halliday Lithograph Corp., West Hanover, Mass.
Designed by David Rogers

Published in the United States of America by
Methuen, Inc.
733 Third Ave.
New York, New York 10017

Contents

THE BOYS FROM LIVERPOOL
John,
Paul,
George,
Ringo

Introducing . . .

During the cold early weeks of 1964, four young musicians who called themselves the Beatles put America under a spell from which it has never recovered. John Lennon, Paul McCartney, George Harrison, and Ringo Starr, already heroes to millions of young Britons and Europeans, became overnight legends in the United States as well. For the rest of the 1960s, the whole of the Western world seemed to move to the magic beat of the four boys from Liverpool, England. Along the way, the sound of popular music changed almost beyond recognition—and with it, the appearance, the style, and the attitudes of young people everywhere.

Many of the reasons for this can be heard in the most fascinating "Beatles story" of all—the one that unfolds when we listen to the remarkable series of records the group made between 1962 and 1970. But unlike other great recording artists, the Beatles were so much more than "just" exceptional musicians and songwriters. Their sudden impact was caused as much by the force of their four personalities as by the music itself.

Ringo Starr was the humblest and most down-to-earth of the Beatles. Like the lovable runt of a litter, he seemed to stir a mothering instinct in female fans. For much of the Beatles' career, Ringo would keep himself somewhat in the background, happy to let the other three handle most of the interviews and singing and songwriting. But when the Beatles first arrived in the United States, the five-foot eight-inch drummer with the big nose, sad expression, and four rings got more attention from reporters than all three of the five-foot-eleven guitarists with the ordinary British names put together.

George Harrison was, in many girls' opinion, the handsomest Beatle. Though the group's finest and most dedicated musician, George still let John and Paul hog most of the limelight onstage as well as off when the Beatles first visited America. Not yet twenty-one at the time, the youngest of the "mop-tops" would prove the last to really emerge as an individual in his own right.

Paul McCartney was the Beatle with the most obvious "star quality." He was also a brilliant public-relations man. Paul himself admits: "I was always the one who would kind of sit the press down and say, 'Hello, how are you? Do you want a drink,' and make them comfortable." George remembers Paul as "the one with a smile, a wave and an autograph. We'd always be sitting in the car waiting for him—'C'mon, Paul!'—and he'd be signing away." The McCartney charm won over many parents, even as those angelic looks played on their daughters' heartstrings. Paul had the most romantic image of the Beatles, but behind the scenes he was also the most hard-working and concerned about what would sell.

John Lennon remained the Beatles' guiding spirit until they finally began to break up. Yet in the first rush of "Beatlemania" he drew fewer screams than the others. This was partly because John was "the married Beatle"—but also because some young girls found his cynicism and brutal honesty a bit scary. To other fans, however, Lennon appeared to personify the word "cool". He also came across as the most intelligent member of the group.

That, in a nutshell, is how the world viewed the individual Beatles in early 1964—once people learned to tell them apart beneath their startling "long hair". The combination of their four personalities and talents was unbeatable. Over the next five or so years, they developed more and more as individuals—to the point that they began to grow apart and finally split up. Ringo

4

changed the least; always the group's "anchor," he remained the simplest and most straightforward of the four. George discovered Indian music and religion, and turned into the Beatles' resident philosopher and mystic. Paul became the band's all-round entertainer and musician, with a knack for writing, playing, and singing music in just about every imaginable style. John began to chronicle his personal life and feelings with a series of groundbreaking, at times earth-shaking, songs—the likes of which nobody had ever before written.

Yet these four extraordinary individuals all came from very ordinary backgrounds. This, in fact, was why millions could identify with them so easily—and continued to follow their every move with such interest. It was as if a group of "boys next door" had hit the jackpot in some fantastic, fairy-tale lottery, winning fortune, fame, and power on an almost unheard-of scale. What these four very human beings did with it makes for one of the amazing stories of their times. . . .

1

"So What's from Liverpool?"
(through 1963)

Some twenty years ago today, a twenty-seven-year-old would-be actor stepped down the seventeen greasy stairs that led into a rock 'n' roll cellar club in Liverpool, England. He had been drawn to the Cavern Club for the first time by a strange whim, but almost immediately wished he hadn't come. "It was as black as a deep grave, damp and dank and smelly," he later remembered. With his well-trimmed hair and well-cut suit, the shy visitor both looked and felt out of place among the scruffy teen-agers in blue jeans.

A few in the milling crowd recognized him as Brian Epstein, the man in charge of the record section of his family's NEMS department store. Wondering what on earth he was doing at the Cavern, one girl started chatting with him. But their conversation and the program of American rock 'n' roll records that all but drowned it out were cut short by the appearance of four leather-jacketed youths on the raised platform at one end of the cellar.

After plugging in and tuning up their cheap electric guitars, the quartet ripped into their first number. It was raw and loud, very different from the mushier sounds that dominated British pop music at the time. To get a better look at the band, Brian later recalled, "I eased myself towards the stage, past rapt faces and jiggling bodies." One of his first impressions of the performers was that "they were not very tidy and not very clean."

By the standards of 1961, they seemed in desperate need of haircuts.

Their onstage conduct also struck Brian as being quite unprofessional. They took long pauses between numbers to tune up, swap private jokes, smoke cigarettes, and eat snacks. But as far as their fans were concerned, these interruptions did not seem to mar the excitement of the show. If anything, the musicians' defiantly individual attitude only added to their appeal. To his surprise, Brian found himself fascinated by the way they looked and sounded, and by the almost magnetic hold they had over their audience.

Most of the singing and talking was handled by two of the group's members. One of these—the twenty-one-year-old rhythm guitar and harmonica player with the cowboy boots—came across as both arrogant and aggressive. His announcements to the crowd, though sarcastic and insulting, and peppered with four-letter words, were hilariously funny. His singing voice was as forceful as his character.

By contrast, the charming twenty-year-old bass guitarist made more of an effort to act the part of the show-business star. Extremely good-looking—some would use the word pretty—he enjoyed flirting with the girls who clustered about the makeshift stage, unable to take their eyes off him. While sharing the rhythm guitarist's ability to belt out hard rockers, the bass player had an equal talent for singing in a very different style. At the drop of a high hat he could switch from a voice as rough as sandpaper for Little Richard's "Long Tall Sally" to that of a romantic crooner tugging at female heartstrings with a honey-tongued version of a Broadway-musical hit song like "Till There Was You."

Between them, the lean and hungry-looking eighteen-year-old lead guitarist tended to hunch over his instrument in concentration when he wasn't singing harmonies or his occasional vocal solo. It was clear that, despite their differing personalities, these three were unusually close, both as musicians and as friends. Behind the guitarists, somewhat out of the picture, a surly-looking drummer pounded away. He, too, got a lot of adoring glances from the young ladies.

At the time, it seemed like just another lunch-hour gig to the four rock 'n' roll musicians named John Lennon, Paul McCartney, George Harrison, and Pete Best. But history would record that afternoon of November 9, 1961—when Brian Epstein first set eyes upon the young ragamuffins who called themselves the Beatles—as the start of the transformation of a band of struggling amateurs into the most successful foursome the world has ever known.

The strange whim that brought the suave record dealer to the seedy, smoke-filled Cavern had grown out of a request a young man had made at the NEMS store twelve days earlier. The youth was searching for a record called "My Bonnie," by a group named the Beatles.

Within two days, more teen-agers had come into the shop, looking for the same mysterious record. His curiosity aroused, Brian set about asking his Liverpool music contacts for information about those strangely spelt Beatles.

He was told that they were local lads, who had just returned from one of several visits to Hamburg, Germany. Their music had stirred up quite a sensation there, and the Beatles had been chosen to back up a British singer named Tony Sheridan in the recording studios. One of the songs they had taped in Hamburg was "My Bonnie," which had been released as a single in Germany. Now the Beatles were back in town, appearing regularly at the Cavern.

All this interested Brian enough to cause him not only to import copies of "My Bonnie" for his shop but, as we have seen, to check out the band's live act as well.

After watching them perform for the first time, he found himself returning to the Cavern again and again. Out of character as this may have seemed, there was a hidden side to Brian's nature that was dissatisfied with his respectable but dull existence. He could not erase the image of those four talented young ruffians from his mind, and soon managed to get on friendly speaking terms with John, Paul, George, and Pete. Within a month, he made a proposal that surprised and pleased them almost as much as it upset his own family: he would become the Beatles' manager.

Brian Epstein stepped into the Cavern and into the Beatles' lives at a time when they desperately wanted to break out of the rut in which they felt trapped. They had become folk heroes in the two grimy ports of Liverpool and Hamburg, but the rest of the world didn't seem to want to know. The boys still counted themselves lucky if they made £15 ($40) a performance. Even the single "My Bonnie" turned out to have billed the group as "the Beat Brothers." The record company had felt that the name "Beatles" would be too confusing for the German market.

Liverpool, England, might at first seem an unlikely birthplace for a musical revolution. The city's moment of glory was long over by World War II, during which all four Beatles were born. There was still much grand architecture from the days when the sun never set on Queen Victoria's British Empire, when ships constantly steamed up the Mersey River, laden with rich cargo from India and Africa and the Caribbean.

But by the time the Beatles were born, the Victorian buildings had become as sooty and run-down as the dreary rows of identical brick tenements that sprawled across most of the city. Even the once-thriving local cotton trade—in which Paul McCartney's father worked—was in a bad state. Many people had no jobs, and those who did had to work very hard to earn very little.

Still, the ships continued to unload their cargo at Liverpool's docks. Even if the money had become tighter, the sailors who arrived from all over the world kept the Merseyside lively. In the fifties, seamen brought in all the latest American rock 'n' roll records, which put Liverpool well ahead of most inland English cities in its awareness of the new music.

Over the years, the port had also seen the arrival of many immigrants. Most of these—including John Lennon's and Paul McCartney's grandparents—came from Ireland, land of minstrels, whose economy was in even worse shape than Liverpool's.

They had to live by their wits to survive in their tough new surroundings, and music was one of the few pleasures many of them could afford. So maybe it is not so surprising after all that rock 'n' roll's gritty beat found its second wind along the muddy Mersey River.

The only Beatle to grow up in a really dismal slum area was Ringo Starr, the eldest and the last to join the group. Richard Starkey (his real name) was born on July 7, 1940, in a house without electricity or indoor plumbing. He was brought up by his mother, who divorced and remarried when he was very little. His family and neighbors remember Richie as an easygoing boy, simple and straightforward but quite sickly. He spent much of his childhood in hospitals, and as a result got very little formal education.

Richie eventually acquired the nickname "Ringo," thanks perhaps to his habit of wearing four or five rings all the time. He also developed a keen interest in the American West—in cowboys, and in country music—and at one point applied for a job in Houston, Texas. Fortunately for the future of rock 'n' roll, young Richard Starkey's request was turned down. Instead, he pursued his hobby of playing the drums in Liverpool bands.

John Lennon was born on October 9, 1940. Neither of his parents was very stable or responsible, and Aunt Mimi, the sister of John's mother, Julia, took over the boy's upbringing. John's father, a sailor, soon ran off to New Zealand and did not set eyes on his son again until he saw the Beatles on TV in 1964. Though Julia remained in Liverpool, the no-nonsense Aunt Mimi tended to keep John away from his offbeat mother until he reached his teens.

Perhaps the dramatic breakup of his family contributed to what John would describe in one of his songs as "a chip on my shoulder that's bigger than my feet." He became his school's leading troublemaker and failed all his subjects except art. His report cards featured such comments as "hopeless," "a clown in class," and "just wasting other students' time."

Even so, John was convinced he was a genius: "I always wondered, 'Why has nobody discovered me?' Didn't they see that I was cleverer than anybody in this school? That the teachers are stupid too? That all they had was information I didn't need? I was different, I was always different. But they were trying to beat me into being a dentist or a teacher."

All his schoolmasters were sure he would come to a bad end, except for one who recognized his unusual talent and helped get him into art college. But John Lennon was clearly the type of person who could never conform to the expectations of schools or other institutions. On his own, he loved to read, but the books that interested him were seldom the ones his teachers assigned. His favorite was Lewis Carroll's *Alice in Wonderland*.

John also enjoyed writing and illustrating his own humorous poems and stories. "I used to say to me auntie, 'You throw my poetry out and you'll regret it when I'm famous'—and she threw the stuff out." But in 1956, when Elvis Presley became a worldwide star, John discovered an even greater passion—the guitar. Now his two secret ambitions were "to write an *Alice in Wonderland* and be bigger than Elvis." While still in art school, he formed his own band, called the Quarrymen.

Aunt Mimi strongly disapproved of this new hobby. But Julia Lennon—whom John was finally getting to know better—encouraged her teen-age son in this and all his other rebellious habits. Mrs. Lennon's role was less that of a parent than of a rather naughty older sister, taking part in John's outrageous routines and practical jokes.

In 1957, Julia Lennon was run over and killed by a car, just outside the house where Aunt Mimi and John lived. Though outwardly, as always, John showed little emotion, inside he felt torn apart. Eleven years later, on the Beatles' "White Album," he would finally reveal his deeply tender feelings for his mother in the beautiful "song of love for Julia." But at the time, as far as the rest of the world could tell, John only became more obnoxious than ever, humiliating all but a few close friends with his sharp, cruel wit.

One of these friends was Paul McCartney, who by this time

The Beatles at Liverpool's Cavern Club in 1961. *From left to right:*
Paul McCartney, John Lennon, Pete Best, and George Harrison

At the age of sixteen, John (*center*) fell under the
spell of Elvis Presley and formed his first band

George Harrison as a
young teen-ager, with
his first guitar

Ringo Starr (*bottom*), the last to join the Beatles, was originally
the drummer for Rory Storme and the Hurricanes (*Rex Features*)

John, George, and Paul at the Cavern Club with their new
drummer, Ringo Starr (*second from right*) (*Globe Photos*)

Paul, George, John, and Ringo at the Liverpool docks, after Brian Epstein
replaced their leather outfits with suits and ties (Keystone Press Agency)

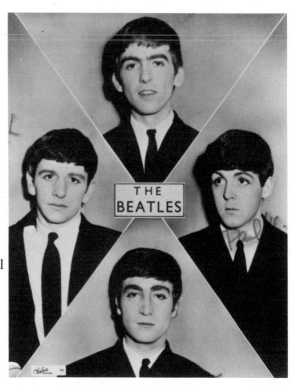

One of the first promotional
pictures of (*clockwise from
left*) Ringo, George, Paul,
and John

"Long hair" and gray collarless suits were part of the Beatles image
that captured Britain's imagination in mid-1963 (*Keystone Press Agency*)

had become a member of the Quarrymen. Paul's mother had also died recently, leaving his father, Jim, to cope with the upbringing of two teen-age boys. Mr. McCartney, who once played piano in a ragtime band, offered more encouragement to the Quarrymen than Aunt Mimi, though he did try to interest them in playing what he considered "good music."

Despite his musical father, James Paul McCartney—born on June 18, 1942—hadn't shown much interest in any instrument until Elvis Presley came along. Then Paul ran out and exchanged the trumpet his dad had given him on his birthday for a guitar. At first he made little headway with it, until he realized that, being left-handed, he needed to have the strings changed around. The fact that Paul held his instrument to the left rather than the right would later give the Beatles a neat visual balance most completely right-handed bands lacked.

Unlike John, Paul was generally polite and charming to his elders, and did quite well at school. He planned to become a teacher when he grew up—until John came along to lead him astray. Though Paul was two years younger, John let him into the Quarrymen because he knew more chords than anyone else in the band. Soon the pair were turning out "Lennon-McCartney originals" like "One After 909" and "Love Me Do." This flair for writing their own music would be one of the things that would set the Beatles apart from other struggling Liverpool groups.

Before long, Paul brought an even younger friend into the Quarrymen, who turned out to be the best guitarist of them all. This was George Harrison, born on February 25, 1943, son of a local bus conductor. John's friends did not take to him at first; he seemed so young, and less obviously clever than Paul. John himself admits: "I couldn't be bothered with George when he first came around. He used to follow me around like a bloody kid, hanging around all the time. It took me years to start considering him as an equal or anything."

But aside from the new Quarryman's dedication to music—he would practice the guitar until his fingers bled—George had something else in his favor. This was his mother, Louise, who has been called one of the world's born fans. She encouraged the boys to practice in her home, where they also could always count on large helpings of Mrs. Harrison's cooking, and she attended all their local performances. Once George and his group became world-famous, Louise Harrison would cheerfully answer dozens of fan letters a day. By that time, none of the other relatives, or the Beatles themselves, could be bothered even to read the mountains of fan mail.

The other Quarrymen gradually faded out of the picture, leaving only John, Paul, and George. The three guitarists began a long search for a bass player and a drummer. John finally persuaded his best friend from art college, Stuart Sutcliffe, to buy a bass and join the band.

Stu was an extremely talented painter whose work had already won prizes in Liverpool. In some people's opinion he was the most intelligent and sensitive of all the Beatles. But music never really became one of his strong points. The group lost many chances to perform because they refused to replace Stu with another bassist. This is one example of the loyalty they felt for each other, and the "us-against-the-world" attitude that they had developed. No slick promoter was going to change the lineup of *their* band.

Finding a drummer proved more difficult. "We had all sorts of different drummers all the time," Lennon remembers, "because people who owned drum kits were few and far between; it was an expensive item. They were usually idiots." The boys at long last settled on quiet, moody-looking Pete Best, whose mother ran a club called the Casbah. Pete's inclusion in the group, therefore, gave them a regular place to perform, though soon they were playing at the larger Cavern as well. They also began to pick up more and more engagements at dance halls around the city, where their shows were often the site of bloody brawls between Liverpool's violent teen-age gangs.

After a period of calling his band Johnny and the Moondogs, Lennon popped up with the name by which they would become famous. One of his heroes was Buddy Holly, the brilliant

American rock 'n' roll star who had recently died in a plane crash at the age of twenty-two. Holly's band had been called the Crickets, so John tried to dream up an insect name for his own act. He hit upon "Beetles," and then, always unable to resist a pun, changed the "Beet" to "Beat." "When you said it," John explained, "people thought of crawly things, when you read it it was beat music."

Except for their weird name and their leader's strong personality, there was still little to set the Beatles apart from the dozens of other teen-age groups playing Liverpool's cellar cafes. The first real test came in 1960, when their unofficial manager, Allan Williams, drove them to Germany in a van to play Hamburg's Reeperbahn. American rock 'n' roll had become very popular in Germany. Because of the difficulties involved in bringing acts all the way from the United States, the Germans were willing to settle for English bands as the next best thing.

The port of Hamburg was, in many ways, Germany's Liverpool. But it was twice as big and twice as tough and dangerous. The Reeperbahn was the worst section of all, known the world over for its violence and vice. Yet here, among the sleazy bars and strip clubs, the Beatles were destined to get their first small taste of fame.

When the Beatles first arrived at the Indra Club, their prospects seemed very depressing. They found that for mere pennies they were expected to play up to eight hours at a stretch. Their meals would be endless bowls of cornflakes, and their sleeping quarters a grimy little dressing room next to the toilets at the back of the club.

It was a sink-or-swim situation, and the Beatles rose to the challenge. With Liverpool so many hundreds of miles away, running home to their parents' apron strings was out of the question. Anyway, to come to Hamburg they had sacrificed college and jobs once and for all. John, Paul, George, Stu, and Pete bravely faced down audiences of drunken sailors, young toughs, and gangsters, all of whom expected a good run for their money. They wanted a real show.

19

The Beatles quickly learned how to give it to them. They writhed and stomped for hours on end, splashing beer over one another and the spectators between songs. John, sometimes wearing a broken toilet seat around his neck, would impersonate Adolf Hitler in fake German. The drunken riffraff of the Reeperbahn loved every minute. They began to pack the Indra Club each night, and when the Beatles moved on to the larger Kaiserkeller, the rowdy fans followed.

But soon the shows started to draw a smarter, classier crowd as well. Young intellectuals from Hamburg's universities became just as spellbound as the leather boys and the sailors. The Beatles began to make friends with young local artists such as Klaus Voorman, who years later would design their *Revolver* LP cover, and Astrid Kirchherr, who before long became engaged to marry Stu Sutcliffe.

The Beatles also grew friendly with another Liverpool band called Rory Storme and the Hurricanes—and especially with the drummer, Ringo Starr, who shared the Beatles' down-to-earth wit. Members of both groups are said to have taken part in the incident that would bring the Beatles' Hamburg stay to an abrupt end.

The musicians had often complained about the dangerously flimsy stage they had to perform on. When it was destroyed by a mysterious fire, the management called in the police. Paul and Pete were fingered as suspects, jailed for a night, and put on the morning flight to England. "The first time I'd flown," says Paul. George was also expelled from the country when it was discovered that he was only seventeen, a year younger than the legal age for nightclub performers.

All five Beatles returned separately to Liverpool, in disgrace and disarray, and in decidedly dismal spirits. With his amplifier on his back, John staggered into Aunt Mimi's house at two in the morning. But when at last the boys pulled their act back together, they found that the long hard hours demanded of them in Hamburg had done wonders for their musicianship and stage presence. The Beatles' Liverpool following rapidly grew as large and enthusiastic as the one they had picked up in Hamburg. In 1961 they would be voted Liverpool's Number One group in a poll conducted by *Mersey Beat*, the local music weekly. Years later, Paul McCartney admitted: "We bought a few copies ourselves and filled them in."

After George turned eighteen in early 1961, the Beatles returned to Hamburg to play at the Kaiserkeller's main competitor, the Top Ten Club. This was the trip on which they first entered a recording studio, to back up Tony Sheridan on "My Bonnie" and five other songs. They also taped their own version of the 1920s hit "Ain't She Sweet," sung by John, and an instrumental composed by John and George called "Cry for a Shadow."

Also on this trip, Astrid talked Stu into changing his greased-back hairstyle to the floppy bangs worn by Klaus Voorman and his student and artist friends. Despite their initial scorn, John, Paul, and George were soon sporting the same look. Thus was the "Beatle hairstyle" born.

When it came time for the Beatles to return to Liverpool with their new hairstyles, Stu remained behind with Astrid. He had come to realize that he had more to offer as a painter than as a musician. Paul took over on bass, and henceforth the Beatles would be a four-man band. Because they hardly needed two rhythm guitarists anyway, the music didn't suffer from the change.

In one of fate's crueler twists, the boy who had been widely viewed as the most sensitive and intelligent Beatle had barely a year left to live. After a long series of violent headaches, Stu Sutcliffe died the following April of a brain tumor—at the age of twenty-one.

The Beatles' lineup was in for another change soon after Brian Epstein entered the picture. John, Paul, and George gave their new manager the dirty job of telling Pete that they wished to replace him with Ringo Starr. The three original Beatles had come to feel that Pete had never really fitted in, and some say that Paul and George were also jealous of his good looks and popularity. At the height of the Beatles' fame, their ex-drummer would wind up slicing bread at a Liverpool bakery for about $50 a week.

Much of the Beatles' local following was furious at Pete's dismissal. Crowds gathered outside the Cavern, chanting "Pete forever, Ringo never." George got a black eye from a group of Best fans, and a bodyguard had to be hired to protect Brian Epstein from the angry gangs. "Overnight," Epstein wrote, "I became the most disliked man on the seething beat scene."

Pete Best and his fans had good reason to feel bitter. Brian Epstein's painstaking efforts to interest record companies in his act had finally begun to pay off.

Brian had been making the rounds in London with a tape John, Paul, George, and Pete had recorded for Decca Records in January 1962. Despite an initial flicker of interest, the people at Decca wound up giving Brian the discouraging message he was destined to hear from so many other record companies as well: "Rock 'n' roll groups are on the way out, Mr. Epstein. You have a good record business in Liverpool. Stick to that." Nobody was the least bit impressed by Brian's insistence that "one day these boys will be bigger than Elvis Presley."

Part of Brian and the Beatles' problem was people's snobbery. Almost nobody in the huge sophisticated city of London could imagine anything new and exciting coming out of a place like Liverpool. "Liverpool?" gasped Dick James, the man who would eventually publish the Lennon-McCartney songs. "You're joking. So what's from Liverpool?" "We were looked down upon as animals by the southerners, the Londoners," Lennon remembers. "We were hicksville."

But finally Brian caught the ear of George Martin, the elegant producer and talent scout for Parlophone Records. Though part of EMI, Britain's biggest record company, Parlophone itself was not doing so well and was in danger of going out of business. Martin had had some success producing Peter Sellers' comedy records, but he was desperate for new acts and willing to give the Beatles a chance.

In June they trooped down to London for their Parlophone audition. Martin found that the group shared his sense of humor. John, especially, was a great admirer of his work with Peter Sellers. But most important, Martin liked the Beatles' sound.

The boys were off on yet another trip to Hamburg when at last the magic telegram from Brian Epstein came: EMI CONTRACT SIGNED SEALED TREMENDOUS IMPORTANCE TO US ALL WONDERFUL. . . . On September 11, 1962, they were back in London to tape their first Parlophone single. Ringo had been in the drummer's seat just a month.

"Let me know if there's anything you don't like," said George Martin kindly as he showed the lads into the studio.

"Well, for a start," George Harrison shot back, "I don't like your tie."

Though their dry sense of humor hadn't suffered any, the Beatles were nervous—especially Ringo. To his dismay, he found that a professional studio drummer had been hired for the session. As Martin wasn't going to take any chances on a drummer he had never heard, poor Ringo was left to rattle a tambourine.

In an age when very few groups wrote their own material, Martin felt that if the Beatles were to score a big hit, they would need to rely on tunes by slick professional songwriters. But because he didn't have anything suitable on hand at the time, Martin was willing to let them do two of John and Paul's own numbers on the first single. These were "Love Me Do" and "PS: I Love You."

"Love Me Do," though hardly an earthshaking song, was chosen because Martin thought John's harmonica solo was an unusual gimmick for a pop record. It was released on October 5, and did better than almost anyone had expected. Thanks to very heavy sales in the Liverpool area, "Love Me Do" eventually reached number seventeen on Britain's national best-seller chart.

Meanwhile, Brian Epstein was doing his best to give the Beatles a more professional and wholesome image. The leather jackets were replaced by matching suits and ties, until Brian finally hit upon the gray collarless jackets in which the Beatles would become world-famous. He did away with the salty stage announcements, the long interruptions, and onstage horseplay. To the typed notes he sent them, giving instructions on upcoming shows, Brian would add such postscripts as: "Note that on ALL the above engagements, during the performances, smoking, eating, chewing, and drinking is STRICTLY PROHIBITED."

All this was fine with Paul, but John sometimes worried that they were selling out. "In the beginning," he has said, "it was a constant fight between Brian and Paul on one side, and me and George on the other. Brian put us in neat suits and shirts, and Paul was right behind him. I didn't dig that, and used to try and get George to rebel with me. I'd say to him: 'Look, we don't need these suits. Let's chuck them out the window.' My little rebellion was to have my tie loose, with the top button of my shirt undone, but Paul would always come up to me and put it straight."

The Beatles were rapidly turning into the cheery and clean-cut "moptops" the whole world would soon know and love. Still based in Liverpool (they moved to London in late 1963), the group plunged into a nonstop series of national tours. The Beatles consistently stole the show from the long-since-forgotten acts that topped the bill at these concerts. The wild escapades of the not-so-distant past were kept secret from the press and the new fans.

John's life was changing in other ways. On August 23, 1962, he became the first Beatle to marry. His bride, Cynthia Powell, was a quiet, sensible blonde he had met in art college. Julian Lennon—named after John's mother—was born the following April. The wedding remained a secret for months.

Encouraged by the modest success of "Love Me Do," George Martin searched for a song that could take the Beatles all the way to the top. He finally settled on Mitch Murray's "How Do You Do It?"

But when the Beatles heard the tune, they told him that they neither liked it nor wished to record it. Martin was amazed at the nerve of these inexperienced young Liverpudlians who could neither read nor write musical notation. He made them tape "How Do You Do It?" anyway. The Beatles, however, played it so poorly that it could never be released.

"You're turning down a hit," Martin scolded them. "It's your funeral, but if you're going to be so stubborn, you'd better produce something better yourselves."

Like magicians pulling a rabbit out of a hat, John and Paul popped up with "Please Please Me," easily their strongest song so far. Even George Martin was impressed.

"Please Please Me" had all the ingredients of the sound that would make the Beatles famous—the rich harmonies, the catchy melodies, the thunderous beat that never lets up for an instant. Within five weeks after its January 1963 release, "Please Please Me" hit Number One all over Britain. The Beatles had arrived. ("How Do You Do It?" was eventually given to another Liverpool group that Epstein had signed on, Gerry and the Pacemakers. It also went to Number One.)

It was now time for the Beatles to make an album. Despite their success on the charts, they were forced to record the whole LP in a single day—February 11, 1963—with two of the group suffering from bad colds.

The *Please Please Me* album contained four new Lennon-McCartney songs. The most popular were "I Saw Her Standing There" and "Do You Want to Know a Secret?" This last was soon recorded by another of Brian Epstein's Liverpool clients, Billy J. Kramer. His version of "Secret" eventually replaced the single of "Please Please Me" as Britain's Number One hit.

Kramer's success with "Do You Want to Know a Secret?" proved that John and Paul were outstanding composers in their own right, whose music could sound good—and sell well—in the hands of other artists. Soon groups from all over the country were begging for new Lennon-McCartney material. One of these was a scruffy fivesome from the London area called the Rolling Stones—whose first hit would be Lennon-McCartney's "I Wanna Be Your Man."

The rest of the Beatles' first album—eventually released in the United States as *Introducing the Beatles* and then *The Early Beatles*— consisted of American songs they had long featured in their performances. As would be the case on later LPs, each Beatle got to sing lead on at least one number. George handled Carole King's "Chains," and even the new drummer had his moment in the spotlight with the Shirelles' "Boys." But most people's favorite was a rip-roaring version of the Isley Brothers' recent U.S. hit "Twist and Shout," sung by John. The Beatles recorded it almost as an afterthought when Martin told them they had enough time left to try one more song.

Please Please Me was soon Britain's Number One album. So it remained for thirty weeks, until another Beatles LP arrived to take its place. A third single, "From Me To You"—which John and Paul had dreamed up in a van on the way to work one evening—also hit the top. As on the first two hits, John's trademark harmonica was the lead instrument. "Then we dropped it," Lennon remembers. "It got embarrassing."

That August the Beatles introduced an even more memorable trademark with their fourth single, "She Loves You." This was the famous "yeah, yeah, yeah" chorus, chanted repeatedly and insistently enough to drive any listener out of his or her mind, for better or for worse. "She Loves You" not only rocketed straight to Number One—it became the biggest selling record *ever* released in Britain (which it remained until 1977 when it was finally outsold by a song called "Mull of Kintyre" by a fellow named Paul McCartney). "She Loves You" also established the Beatles as stars all over Europe and the English-speaking world—except in the United States.

For months the Beatles had been all over the front pages of Britain's weekly music newspapers like *Melody Maker* and *New Musical Express*. Dozens of Beatle fan magazines had appeared on the newsstands to compete with the official *Beatles Monthly Book*, which had been founded in April 1963. Membership in the Beatles Fan Club was nearing a hundred thousand.

Big American stars were now having to settle for second-billing on the Beatles' tours. To get tickets to the shows, teen-agers thought nothing of waiting in line on the streets, with their sleeping bags and umbrellas, for forty-eight hours or more. The Beatles could not go near the concert halls without bodyguards or police escorts for fear of being torn to pieces by the fans. When they appeared onstage, their music was drowned out by screams. They themselves were showered with toys, articles of female clothing, and jelly beans—once their favorite candy, but not for long.

Yet it was not until "She Loves You" that people outside the pop-music world paid much attention to the Beatles craze. However, it was impossible for anyone to ignore the Beatles' October 13 appearance on a nationally televised show at the London Palladium. The hysteria in the theatre and riots on the streets outside were beamed into the living rooms of millions of Britons. Almost overnight, the world "Beatlemania" appeared on page one of every daily newspaper.

Suddenly all of Britain seemed to go bananas over the Beatles. Politicians, priests, psychiatrists, headmasters, and newspaper editors all had something to say about Beatlemania one way or the other. Some attacked or dismissed the craze, but many proclaimed themselves fans of the merry lads from Liverpool.

The Beatles became the first rock 'n' rollers ever to break the age and class barriers. Many parents and younger siblings seemed almost as enthusiastic as the teen-agers, and the Beatles proved to be equally popular with debutantes and factory girls.

John, Paul, George, and Ringo were even invited to perform for the queen's sister and mother at the Royal Variety Show. Before closing with "Twist and Shout," John announced: "For our last number, I'd like to ask your help. Would the people in the cheaper seats clap your hands? And the rest of you, if you'd just rattle your jewelry. . . ."

The Beatles' wit, cheeky but harmless, had a lot to do with their wide appeal. The Queen Mother said: "They are so fresh and vital. I simply adore them!" The following day, Britain's most popular newspaper, The Daily Mirror, ran this editorial:

YEAH, YEAH, YEAH!

You have to be a real sour square not to love the nutty, noisy, happy, handsome Beatles.

If they don't sweep your blues away, *brother you're a lost cause.* If they don't put a beat in your feet, *sister you're not living.*

How refreshing to see these rambunctious young Beatles take a middle-aged Royal Variety Performance by the scruff of their necks and have them beatling like teenagers.

The Beatles are whacky. They wear their hair like a mop, but it's WASHED, it's super clean. So is their fresh young act. . . .

GOOD LUCK, BEATLES!

By Christmas time, the Beatles had another single and album in the shops. "I Want to Hold Your Hand" quickly sold almost as many copies as "She Loves You," and *With the Beatles* became the first album ever to sell over a million copies in Britain. Though it contained the same mixture of Lennon-McCartney originals— plus George's first song "Don't Bother Me"—and versions of American hits (including Chuck Berry's "Roll Over Beethoven"), *With the Beatles* was much better than the first LP. The rough edges were mostly gone, and instead of just copying American sounds, the Beatles were now creating a style that was more English, and uniquely their own. "All My Loving," the first Lennon-McCartney tune to become a "standard," was soon recorded by dozens of other musicians.

At the end of the year, the Beatles got their first serious attention from a classical music critic. William Mann of the London *Times* wrote: "The outstanding English composers of 1963 must seem to have been John Lennon and Paul McCartney, the talented young musicians from Liverpool whose songs have been sweeping the country since last Christmas, whether performed by their own group, the Beatles, or by numerous other teams that they also supply with songs." Mann went on to praise the "pandiatonic clusters" in "This Boy" and the "Aeolian cadence" in "Not a Second Time."

The Beatles got a good laugh out of the article, and admitted they had never even heard of pandiatonic clusters or Aeolian cadences before. But Mann's review was yet another sign that just about all resistance to the Beatles in their own country had crumbled.

Now they would attempt a feat that no British pop-music star had ever managed to pull off before—the conquest of America.

2

The Conquest of America
(1964)

For most of 1963, the American record business had proved as tough a nut for Brian Epstein to crack as the English had been a year earlier. Despite all the British Number Ones and sell-out tours, nobody in the United States seemed to want to know about his Beatles. After all, rock 'n' roll music was a purely American invention. Who could possibly care about some English imitation?

Capitol Records, being the American branch of EMI, the Beatles' British record company, had the first chance at all their releases. But Capitol wasn't interested, so "Please Please Me," "From Me to You," "She Loves You," and the first album were put out in the United States by tiny companies like Vee-Jay and Swan. All sank without a trace.

"We didn't think there was a chance," admitted John. "We just didn't imagine it at all; we didn't even bother. Even when we came over to America the first time, we were only coming over to buy LP's."

Nonetheless, the American pop-music scene was desperately waiting for someone new and exciting to come along. The Golden Age of Rock 'n' Roll was long over. Many of the great stars were either dead—like Buddy Holly—or had lost their touch. Others, including Elvis Presley, had turned into slick "adult" entertainers, crooning sappy ballads to the rich and middle-aged in Las Vegas.

Except for some of the black "Motown" groups, few of America's early 1960s pop stars could boast any real originality or vitality. Rock 'n' roll was in danger of dying in the land of its birth. It needed a shot in the arm—and fast.

Then, on November 22, 1963, John F. Kennedy was assassinated. This youthful, dynamic President had been especially popular with young Americans, and his sudden loss may have made them feel an unconscious need for a new hero. In any case, the country's mood was certainly very depressed during the last weeks of 1963. Magazines and the TV news urgently needed some light relief from all the grim coverage of the Kennedy murder. They found it in reports of the strange epidemic of mass silliness that appeared to have sent Mother England right off her rocker.

Time, Life, and *Newsweek* all ran profiles on John, Paul, George, and Ringo. Their hair, at least, seemed good for a laugh. The Associated Press defined their sound as "a weird new kind of music that makes rock 'n' roll seem tame by comparison." Still, the stories all suggested that Beatlemania was a purely British brand of nuttiness. Nobody seemed to think it could ever spread to the United States.

Then someone at Capitol Records thought: Why not? The company decided to release the Beatles' fifth single, "I Want to Hold Your Hand," after all—and to follow it with an edited version of *With the Beatles,* retitled *Meet the Beatles.* Brian Epstein once wrote that he was sure all along that "if the Beatles were to make a record that would sell in America, then 'I Want to Hold Your Hand' was that record." The song was easily the Beatles' most original and electrifying yet, full of subtle shifts in the pounding rhythm.

Brian came to New York that November to arrange for the Beatles' first United States visit. An appearance at Carnegie Hall was scheduled, and the Beatles were booked on Ed Sullivan's popular Sunday night variety television show. Sullivan had seen Beatlemania firsthand on a trip to England, but he agreed to let the Beatles top the bill only after a great deal of haggling with

Epstein. In exchange for this honor, however, he only paid the Beatles $10,000 for their three February 1964 appearances.

As interest grew, Capitol decided to pour a small fortune into a Beatles "crash publicity campaign." Balding Capitol executives were photographed wearing Beatle wigs, and girls who worked for the company were encouraged to accept free "Beatle hair-do's." Five million stickers reading "The Beatles Are Coming" mysteriously turned up on walls, lamp posts, and phone booths across the fifty states. A million Beatle newsletters tumbled off the press.

Capitol even mailed every disc jockey in the country a list of questions and an "open-ended interview" record featuring John, Paul, George, and Ringo's prerecorded answers. This way any DJ could, whenever he wished, give the impression he was conducting a personal interview with the Beatles.

The boys were on tour in Paris at the end of January when they received the stunning news that "I Want to Hold Your Hand," a mere month after its release, had hit Number One all over the United States. What's more, all the earlier American flops had sprung to life and were racing up the record charts as well, and *Meet the Beatles* was reported to be the fastest-selling LP album ever issued in the United States. The jubilant Beatles threw a celebration dinner in Paris's elegant George V hotel, during which even the staid Brian Epstein was photographed clowning around with a chamber pot on his head as he puffed at his victory cigar.

Still, even after the Beatles had boarded their flight to New York on February 7, they weren't totally convinced that their American success wasn't just a temporary fluke. "Since America has always had everything, why should we be over there making money?" Paul asked Phil Spector, the brilliant young record producer who had become one of the Beatles' first American supporters and friends. "They've got their own groups. What are we going to give them that they don't already have?"

Paul needn't have worried. Though on New Year's Day the names John Lennon, Paul McCartney, George Harrison, and

Ringo Starr meant nothing to Americans, already, only five weeks later, millions of them were dancing and swooning in the grip of the most joyous epidemic of mass insanity the country had ever seen.

Wherever one turned the radio dial in New York, there seemed to be no escaping the Beatles' thunderous beat. Between Beatle records, the disc jockeys on local stations like "W-A-Bea-tle-C" counted down the hours and minutes to the group's arrival. "It's thirty-four Beatle degrees outside at eight-thirty Beatle time—just four hours and fifty minutes to go!"

Over four thousand giddy teen-agers cut classes to pack Kennedy Airport's observation deck—where 110 policemen tried to keep them from getting too unruly. "We've never seen anything like this before," said an airport official. "Not even for presidents and kings." It was also the biggest crowd by far that the boys themselves had yet drawn.

When the Beatles finally stepped out of their Pan-Am jet, their American fans' shrieks dwarfed anything the four boys had heard in Britain or Europe. John, Paul, George, and Ringo were whisked through customs as another crowd of teen-agers clawed at the plate-glass windows. Then they gave their first American press conference.

The reporters who had come to the airport to cover this event didn't expect much. They knew from experience that pop-music stars were generally morons or phonies, or both, who rarely had anything interesting to say. But the reporters were in for a surprise.

"Will you sing something for us?" one asked.

"We need money first," John Lennon shot back.

"What's your message for American teen-agers?"

"Our message," said Paul McCartney, "is buy more Beatle records."

Whatever the question, at least one of the four was sure to be ready with a sharp answer. As The New York Times correspondent put it, "The Beatle wit became contagious. Everyone guffawed. The show was on—and the Beatle boys loved it."

"What about the movement in Detroit to stamp out the Beatles?" demanded another reporter.

"We're starting a movement to stamp out Detroit," said Paul.

"Why do you wear so many rings on your fingers?" Ringo was asked.

"Because I can't get them through my nose."

"Don't you guys ever get a haircut?"

"I just had one yesterday," replied George Harrison. Added Ringo, "You should have seen him the day before."

The United States' first attack of Beatlemania was an experience that will never be forgotten by anyone involved. The fans, of course, had a great time; but—in America more than in Britain—many parents, policemen, and commentators were disgusted at the hysteria, the loud music, and above all, what they felt was the four boys' shockingly long hair.

Nobody was more upset than the management of the Plaza, one of Manhattan's most conservative, expensive, and high-class hotels. When the Beatles' suites had been reserved a month before, the Hotel Plaza had been as unfamiliar as most Americans with the names Lennon, McCartney, Harrison, and Starr, and had assumed they were just another group of decent British businessmen. When the truth finally dawned, the Plaza desperately—and unsuccessfully—tried to find the quartet rooms elsewhere. Throughout the rock 'n' rollers' New York stay, the hotel was exposed to all the wild elements of Beatlemania—including swarms of disc jockeys, reporters, and cameramen, plus the hundreds of screaming fans who camped outside at all hours, kept at bay by several lines of barricades and dozens of policemen.

Most Americans got their first taste of the Beatles in action on the February ninth "Ed Sullivan Show." Though the group was nervous—and George Harrison had come down with the flu—the eight hundred lucky Beatlemaniacs in the studio audience more than made up for the rough edges in their idols' performance. They were well aware that their names had been chosen from sixty thousand ticket requests; even Elvis Presley's famous appearance on Sullivan's show had only drawn seven thousand.

Over seventy million Americans tuned in that night—a record audience for a TV entertainment program. Most did so purely out of curiosity, "to find out what all the fuss was about." Few had ever seen a spectacle such as that offered by the long-haired boys from Liverpool and their crazed fans. Millions of the younger viewers, at least, were completely hooked. By the time the show was over, Beatlemania had swept into the most remote corners of the North American continent.

New York's *Daily News* reported the next morning: "From the moment the Beatles began by blasting out 'All My Loving,' the kids bounced like dervishes in their seats to the driving beat. With the Beatle bounce, performed best by wild-eyed girls aged between 10 and 15, but also likely to infect adults, goes a wild screaming as if Dracula had just appeared on stage. The screams reached a pitch dangerous to the eardrums at times when the Beatles shook their shaggy locks."

On February 11 the Beatles traveled to the nation's capital, to perform their first American concert at the Washington Coliseum. After the show, they appeared as guests of honor at a formal charity ball at the British Embassy. Many of Washington's top socialites were there, some armed with scissors with which to snip away locks of the Beatles' famous hair for souvenirs. John Lennon left early in disgust.

The next day the group was forced to return to New York by train, as a snowstorm had grounded all air traffic. Two separate crowds, each numbering in the thousands, welcomed them at Pennsylvania Station and the Hotel Plaza. "In the shrieking pandemonium," reported the *Daily News*, "one girl was knocked down and trampled, another fainted, and a police sergeant was kicked by a horse. At times the cops could not control the mobs, and the Beatle-lovers broke through barricades in wild assaults in the station and the hotel."

The boys were back in town for a pair of concerts at elegant Carnegie Hall. The management, like that of the Plaza, had had little idea of what they were in store for when the shows were booked in late 1963. Rock 'n' rollers, such as Elvis Presley, had always been refused permission to play there. According to *The New York Times*, the show lasted just thirty-four minutes, after which "all four Beatles fled amid a hail of jelly beans. During this time the Beatles appeared to be singing and playing 12 songs," all of them drowned out by fans "who paid from $3 to $5.50 for the privilege of outshrieking their idols."

The following day, to the great relief of the Hotel Plaza and the New York Police Department, the Beatles flew to Miami to spend the last ten days of their visit on what Brian Epstein had originally planned as a holiday in the sun. But the mobs of cameramen, reporters, and fans gave them little chance to relax. In Florida, the group also did their other two Ed Sullivan shows before flying back to London on February 22.

The Beatles' conquest of the United States was accomplished in one lightning attack—over, it seemed, almost before it got underway. Quite aside from their musical talent, the Beatles appealed to Americans because they seemed so strange, and yet at the same time so real. Their long hair and their Britishness made them appear refreshingly unusual in comparison with earlier American pop stars—but so did the fact that they were intelligent and honest human beings.

Their manager may have tamed them somewhat before they hit the big time, but the Beatles did not by any means come across as the sort of slick, unthinking phonies who had dominated the teen-age music world for far too long. John, Paul, George, and Ringo were no puppets going through the motions while some sharp behind-the-scenes promoter pulled the strings. Unlike the other early-sixties stars, the Beatles spoke their own minds and even drank and smoked in public. Yet they won over many critics with their charm and wit, and their refusal to take themselves or their fame seriously.

The fact that John and Paul wrote most of the Beatles' songs themselves offered further proof that the group was running its own show. Not only did the music sound good, but the words—unlike those dished up by the Tin Pan Alley professionals—

The Beatles shown arriving at New York's Kennedy Airport on February 7, 1964, for their overnight conquest of the American music scene (*Globe Photos*)

Brian Epstein (*left*) introduces John, Ringo, and Paul to Ed Sullivan—on whose TV show most Americans would catch their first glimpse of the Beatles in action (*Popperfoto*)

Ringo, John, Paul, and George talking to American
radio listeners from the Hotel Plaza (*Popperfoto*)

Beatles merchandise on display
in a New York shop window
(*Rex Features*)

Paul McCartney
unwinding in Miami
(*Dezo Hoffman, Rex Features*)

The "Around the Beatles" TV special featured the boys
from Liverpool in a scene from Shakespeare (*Popperfoto*)

John, George, Paul, and
Ringo during a break from
filming their highly praised
first movie, *A Hard Day's
Night* (*Rex Features*)

The "Fab Four" dressed up as Eskimos for
their 1964 Christmas shows (*Rex Features*)

spoke to kids in their own language. Even if the message was still one of teen-age puppy love, the Beatles' use of such everyday phrases as "you know what I mean" in place of the usual tired moon/June rhymes made it ring far more true.

The Beatles' refusal to put their name on anything that did not meet their high standard of quality was also unusual for the time. Before the Beatles came along, the only songs most pop stars cared about were the A sides of their singles. B sides and album tracks were considered to be mere filler, for which any old junk tossed off on the spur of the moment would serve. But far from releasing LPs containing two or three hit singles, padded out with nine "throwaways," the boys from Liverpool just about invented the idea of a completely listenable rock 'n' roll album. What's more, many of their singles became two-sided hits because both songs turned out to be so good.

Not only did each Beatle song have something going for it—so did each Beatle. This, too, was extraordinary at a time when rock 'n' roll bands usually consisted of one "star" backed by a bunch of faceless sidemen. The four Beatles were all stars, distinct characters and talents who each added something special to the group's appeal. Beatlemaniacs had their choice of four different heroes, all of whom acquired a huge individual following. The group's range of personalities seemed to offer something for almost everybody.

But some Americans—especially older ones—did not find anything appealing about any of the Beatles. The day they arrived, Chet Huntley announced on the NBC Evening News: "Like a good little news organization we sent three cameramen out to Kennedy Airport today. However, after surveying the film our men returned with, and the subject of that film, I feel there is absolutely no need to show any of that film."

Evangelist Billy Graham dismissed the Beatles as "a passing phase." The New York *World Telegram* labeled their music "a haunting combination of rock 'n' roll, a hungry cat riot, and Fidel Castro on a harangue."

A right-wing Christian crusader, the Reverend David A. Noebel, went so far as to call Beatlemania a Communist plot "to make a generation of American youth mentally ill and emotionally unstable" and "prepare them for future submission to subversive control." When told about this, Paul McCartney exclaimed: "Us, Communists? Why, we can't be Communists. We're the world's number one capitalists!"

Such crackpot theories aside, the most controversial thing about the Beatles was their hair. Nowadays we look at photographs from that first visit, and it is hard to see what all the fuss was about. The Beatles' hair back then wasn't much longer than, say, President Carter's is now. But as John Lennon remembers, "When we got here you were all walkin' around in Bermuda shorts with Boston crewcuts. We just thought, what an ugly race." Paul McCartney has put it this way: "There they were in America, all getting housetrained for adulthood with their indisputable principle of life: short hair equals men, long hair equals women. Well, we got rid of that convention for them. And a few others, too."

In early 1964, that "principle of life" was so much a part of American adults' thinking that most considered the Beatles' hair to be a very strange gimmick—at best ridiculous, at worst disgusting. Beatle wigs soon became the best-selling novelty since yo-yos, and cartoonists and retouch artists had a field day producing Beatle-browed pictures of current celebrities and politicians.

Some Americans just couldn't believe that the Beatles' hair was actually real. "A photographer asked us if he could take two pictures of us," said Paul. "One with our wigs on and one with our wigs off." During a press conference when the group was asked, "How do you feel about teen-agers imitating you with Beatle wigs?" John snapped back, "They're not imitating us because we don't wear Beatle wigs."

Boys did, however, begin imitating the Beatles by growing their hair as long as parents and teachers would let them. In most cases, that wasn't very long by today's standards. For the rest of the sixties, long hair on males would become a symbol of rebellion against adult society, and one of the burning issues in the battle between the generations. Until the early seventies, a long-haired boy could rarely walk down an American street without being called nasty names.

The Beatle wig was only one of over a hundred different Beatle products offered for sale during the first months of 1964. There were Beatle brands of just about every kind of clothing and jewelry, stationery and toy, and even of junk food. From the lunch boxes, bubble-gum cards, and "long-eating liquorice records" to the Milton-Bradley "Flip Your Wig" board game, the pink plastic guitars, and the beetle-shaped jewelry (in the early days the group's name always brought to mind the creepy-crawly things; now it's the other way around)—all told, Americans snapped up Beatle trinkets to the tune of over $50 million in 1964 alone. "Anytime you spell Beatle with an 'a' in it," gloated Ringo, "we get some money."

The American market was also swamped by literally dozens of Beatle records, some of which were complete rip-offs. Vee-Jay Records, having lost the group to Capitol, recycled the first album with three different covers and titles. The Tony Sheridan recordings that the boys had played on in Hamburg were issued—under the Beatles' name, of course—on a half dozen different LPs. Four unofficial Beatle interview albums also turned up in record stores. There was even a budget-priced album called *The Beetle Beat*, featuring bad imitations of the Beatles' hits by an unknown group. The cover looked so much like that of *Meet the Beatles* that thousands of unsuspecting fans were conned into buying it.

When Capitol announced a March 16 release date for "Can't Buy Me Love," the next official Beatles single, a record-breaking two million advance orders poured in. The company's *Beatles' Second Album*—a mishmash containing "She Loves You," a handful of single B sides, and the American rock 'n' roll songs that had been left off *Meet the Beatles*—became the first LP in the United States ever to reach Number One within two weeks of its release.

The Beatles' grip upon the American record business was so strong that on April 4, 1964, the top five hits on *Billboard's* best-selling singles chart were as follows:

1. "Can't Buy Me Love." The Beatles (Capitol).
2. "Twist and Shout." The Beatles (Tollie).
3. "She Loves You." The Beatles (Swan).
4. "I Want to Hold Your Hand." The Beatles (Capitol).
5. "Please Please Me." The Beatles (Vee-Jay).

The same week, the Beatles were Number One and number two on the LP chart as well. Nobody has ever come close to matching that feat. You may still read all about it in *The Guinness Book of World Records.*

Once the Beatles had so successfully proved that English groups could do well in America after all, the former colonies were flooded with British music and fashions. The mother country became *the* "in" place as far as American youth was concerned. Fan magazines even printed lessons in British teen-age slang—including such Liverpool words as "gear" and "fab" (both of which meant "terrific"). The Beatles themselves came to be known as the Fab Four.

American record companies signed up practically anything that made noise with a British—or, better yet, Liverpool—accent. The British Invasion of 1964 was soon in full swing.

Most of the first groups to follow the Beatles' footsteps were weak imitations like the Dave Clark Five. But before long, talented and exciting bands like the Rolling Stones and The Who would offer the Beatles stiff competition. Shunning suits and ties, and letting their hair fall past their earlobes, groups like the Stones developed images far wilder and more rebellious than the Beatles'.

The Fab Four themselves pressed on with a number of ground-breaking activities. In 1964 John's first book of his own writings and drawings was published. Called *In His Own Write*, it offered solid proof that at least one Beatle's creative talents extended far beyond just writing and singing silly love songs. John's short self-description at the back of the book gives some idea of the wacky wordplay that flavors his writing:

ABOUT THE AWFUL

I was bored on the 9th of Octover 1940 when, I believe, the Nasties were still booming us led by Madalf Heatlump. . . . I attended to varicous schools in Liddypol. And still didn't pass—much to my Aunties supplies.

All Lennon's stories were filled with wild puns like "stabbed undressed envelope," and his characters usually came to a gruesome end. *Newsweek* said that his book "suggests that when John Lennon sings 'I Want to Hold Your Hand' he is wishing he could bite it." But the same review—like many others—ranked the Beatle with Edward Lear and Lewis Carroll in "the English tradition of literary nonsense." All expressed surprise at how good *In His Own Write* was.

John's book bumped James Bond off the top of the best-seller list. The author was invited as guest of honor to a Foyle's Literary Lunch held on Shakespeare's four hundredth birthday and attended by many of Britain's top writers and intellectuals. But John was booed when he refused to give a speech.

"The literary Beatle," as he was called, began collecting material for a second volume, *A Spaniard in the Works.* "I put things down on sheets of paper and stuff them in my pockets," he said. "When I have enough, I have a book."

A project that would convert even more doubters to the Beatles was already underway in March 1964. Work on their first movie would keep John, Paul, George, and Ringo busy for most of the spring. Only at the very end—after the boys had voted down such titles as *Moving On, Let's Go,* and *Beatlemania*—did Ringo pop up with the phrase "A Hard Day's Night." The next morning John and Paul had already written a song to fit the new title.

Plans for a Beatles movie were originally drawn up in the autumn of 1963. Because the group was then little known outside Britain, United Artists put up a budget of a mere half million dollars for a black and white film.

"The idea," said director Richard Lester, "was to make it as quickly as possible and get it out before their popularity faded." Even so, Brian Epstein and the Beatles tried their best to make sure that the film wouldn't turn out to be the sort of corny junk earlier stars like Elvis Presley had made to cash in on their success as recording artists.

"We insisted on having a real writer to write it," said John. They came up with a fellow Liverpudlian named Alun Owen, who had written a TV show about Liverpool that they admired. To take notes for his script, Owen joined the Beatles on a tour of Ireland. "He stayed with us for two days," said John, "and wrote the whole thing based on our characters then: me, witty; Ringo, dumb and cute; George, this; Paul, that." For some scenes, such as the boys' press conference, just about all Owen had to do was write down what he heard.

A Hard Day's Night recreated a day in the life of the Beatles. It was so convincing that it almost seemed like a documentary. But everything was exaggerated just enough to make the film something of a satire on Beatlemania as well. John has said that the Beatles wanted it to be even more realistic, yet he admits, "It was a good projection of us on tour, in a hotel, having to perform before people. We were like that."

In the film, the Beatles travel by train from one city to another, dodging screaming mobs at both ends. They are shown giving press conferences, posing for photographers, making records, and finally, playing the concert that brings the house down and the film to a resounding climax.

These activities may seem exciting to the rest of us. But for a Beatle—in *A Hard Day's Night*, at least—they are merely the everyday routine, to be avoided at every chance. Like their young fans, the Fab Four would rather romp in the fields or flirt with the opposite sex than face up to their responsibilities. Intruders from the phony, uptight adult world are all dealt with with good-natured impertinence.

The stuffy businessman who shares the Beatles' train compartment angrily switches off their transistor radio. "I travel on this train regularly, twice a week," he barks. "I have my rights." In response, John Lennon lisps, "Give us a kiss."

The slick promoter trying to get George to model a shirt tells the Beatle: "You'll like these. You'll really *dig* them. They're *fab.*"

"I wouldn't be seen anywhere in them. They're dead grotty," says George—in the process adding the word *grotty* to the English language.

"Make a note of that word," the promoter whispers to his secretary. "Give it to Susan to use on the show."

"And who's this Susan when she's home?" asks George.

"Only Susan Campey, our resident teen-ager. You'll have to love her. She's your symbol."

"You mean that posh bird who gets everything wrong? She's a drag, a well-known drag. We just turn the sound down on her and say rude things."

From such confrontations, the Beatles always come out on top in high spirits and ready for the next round. But because they never seemed nasty or unpleasant, even older moviegoers couldn't help but root for the cheeky Liverpudlians. "So help me, I resisted the Beatles as long as I could," began one of *A Hard Day's Night*'s thousands of rave reviews. *The New York Times* film critic—no Beatlemaniac—told his adult readers: "This is going to surprise you—it might knock you right out of your chair—but the new film with those incredible chaps the Beatles is a whale of a comedy. I wouldn't believe it myself, if I hadn't seen it with my own astonished eyes."

Director Richard Lester's work in *A Hard Day's Night* is brilliantly imaginative. For instance, during some of the Beatles' songs he shifts the camera angle in time to the music. But Lester's technical excellence would have been wasted had not John, Paul, George, and Ringo proved themselves capable of projecting their full appeal onto the movie screen. The boys' natural talent for slapstick earned many comparisons with the great Marx Brothers.

Ringo Starr was singled out for special praise. Perhaps the most popular scene of all was the one in which Ringo, goaded by Paul's mischievous "grandfather," slips out of the Beatles' camp just before they are due to play their concert. The depressed drummer's riverside encounter with a young schoolboy—who is also playing hooky—deeply moved many viewers. Later Ringo admitted that he only managed to pull the scene off after several strong drinks. Nonetheless, it proved that Ringo had a talent for acting which he would make good use of in years to come.

A Hard Day's Night's opening—at the London Pavilion on July 6, 1964—was a wild, glittering scene that would be repeated for the Beatles' next two movie premieres. Traffic was banned from the area, except for the parade of Rolls-Royces carrying the Fab Four and such glamorous guests as Princess Margaret. A heavily policed and barricaded Piccadilly Circus overflowed with the thousands of Beatlemaniacs out for a glimpse of their idols.

Though the Beatles' records would keep getting better over the next four or five years, they would never improve upon their first movie. *A Hard Day's Night* turned out to be as popular with the public as with the critics. To keep up with the demand from cinemas all over the world, more prints—fifteen thousand in all—were run off of *A Hard Day's Night* than of any other film ever made. United Artists certainly got a good return on its meager investment.

The *Hard Day's Night* LP was also a great success on every level. For the first time, all the songs on the album were Lennon-McCartney originals. Some—especially Paul's beautiful ballad "And I Love Her"—were among the first Beatle tunes to become "standards," performed in every imaginable style by dozens of different music stars all over the world.

The Beatles were improving as recording artists as well as songwriters. Though they had wailed cheerfully out of tune on some of the earlier hits, from now on all their records would be note perfect.

Soon after the film was completed, the Beatles blitzed Holland, Denmark, Hong Kong, Australia, and New Zealand. Though Ringo, stricken by tonsilitis, collapsed in a London photographer's studio just before their scheduled departure, the show had to go on. A drummer named Jimmy Nicol became a Beatle for a week, until the recovered Starr was able to join his three mates in Melbourne. A quarter million people—the largest collection of Australians ever seen in one place—lined the streets for the four Beatles' triumphant reunion.

In August and September, twenty-five North American cities got a firsthand taste of Beatlemania when the Fab Four staged their first cross-country tour. They started in San Francisco, to a ticker-tape reception; and everywhere the Beatles traveled, they encountered the hysterical response they had drawn in New York, Washington, and Miami the previous winter.

John, Paul, George, and Ringo were only four of the many hundreds of people to profit from the Beatle madness. Two of the cleverest hucksters to ride the Beatle bandwagon actually bought—for $1,150—the sheets the boys had slept on from their hotels in Detroit and Kansas City. The precious linen was then cut into 150,000 square-inch sections—which were mounted upon parchment labeled "suitable for framing"—and marketed to American fans for a dollar apiece.

In 1964, entrepreneurs would try just about anything to wring a buck out of Beatlemania before the craze fizzled out. But the Beatles themselves had no intention of fizzling out just yet.

3

Members of the British Empire
(1965)

If 1964 was the year the Beatles conquered the world, it was also probably their most tiring ever. You don't become the biggest recording stars in history without lots of very hard work. In 1964 alone, the Beatles played more than a hundred concerts in ten countries. That's not counting dozens of TV appearances.

Eighteen days after returning from America, the boys began another exhausting five-week tour—this one of England. In those days they had little chance to relax with their families and friends, even between tours. Brian Epstein wanted new Beatle records in the shops by Christmas, when more records are sold than at any other time of the year. So as soon as they got home from America, the Beatles went straight into the recording studio to tape a single and an album.

Back then, John and Paul made up most of their songs either right in the studio or else "on the road," in the hotel rooms where they were virtually prisoners of their own fame, and in the buses and planes that carried them from place to place. Because of the screaming crowds that followed them everywhere and surrounded their hotels, it was usually too complicated for the Beatles to go out and see the sights in the cities they visited. According to Ringo, "It was 24 hours a day without a break. Press, people fighting to get into your hotel room, climbing 25 stories up drainpipes. And it never stopped."

Locked in their rooms, the Beatles had little choice but to play cards and Monopoly and write more hit songs.

Some of the new tunes, like "Eight Days a Week," had the familiar sound of their earlier hits. And, much as today's stars often record Lennon-McCartney tunes, the Beatles also taped some more old favorites by the early rock 'n' roll stars who had been their own heroes in the fifties.

But the boys' new album—called *Beatles '65* in America and *Beatles For Sale* elsewhere—offered as well a hint of a quality that would keep John, Paul, George, and Ringo at Number One in the charts and in the hearts of millions until the day they broke up. This was their refusal to rest on their laurels, to keep doing the same old thing that had made them famous. By constantly changing and growing, in their words and music and everything else they did, the Beatles would keep the world interested. Everyone always wondered what they would come up with next.

For example, when the Beatles first made it big, nobody took the words to their songs seriously—especially not John and Paul, who wrote them. "To express myself," John would remember in interviews years later, "I would write *Spaniard in the Works* or *In His Own Write*, stories which were expressive of my personal emotions. I'd have a separate songwriting John Lennon and I didn't consider the lyrics to have any depth at all. That got embarrassing, and I began writing about what happened to *me*."

By the end of 1964, John was already beginning to express his feelings a bit more openly and honestly in his songs. "I'm not a tough guy," he admitted long afterward. "I always had a facade of being tough to protect myself. But really I'm a sensitive, weak guy." In "I'm a Loser," he sang that though he might "act like a clown," beneath his mask he was "wearing a frown."

While recording another of his new compositions, "I Feel Fine," John liked the sound he heard when he accidentally produced feedback with his electric guitar. The Beatles decided to use this strange buzz, so unmusical by the standards of 1964 AM radio, at the beginning of the record itself.

This was one of the first of many examples of the Beatles' willingness to experiment with previously unheard-of sounds and ideas. Jimi Hendrix and The Who went on to make feedback an important part of late-sixties rock. They probably heard it on the radio at the end of 1964, when "I Feel Fine" became the Beatles' newest Number One record.

On other songs from this period, the Beatles started to depart from the simple two guitars-bass-and-drums sound of their stage act and early albums. They began to show an interest in different instruments, which would increase over the next few years. Aside from more piano and organ, you can hear Ringo playing timpani (large kettledrums) on "Every Little Thing." On Buddy Holly's "Words of Love" he got the sound he wanted by drumming on an old suitcase.

American fans might object that those two songs weren't on *Beatles '65*. True; so maybe we should mention one of the confusing things about collecting Beatle records. Until *Sgt. Pepper's Lonely Hearts Club Band* came out in 1967, the albums in America had different songs and often different titles, from those in England and Europe.

The Beatles' English LPs usually contained fourteen songs, the American ones only eleven. Furthermore, the hit singles, like "I Feel Fine," were generally included on the U.S. album but not on the British. In this manner Capitol, the Beatles' American record company, was able to save up leftover songs and put out extra albums. By the summer of 1966 there were eleven different Beatle albums out in the United States and only seven in England. Capitol Records made more money that way. They knew American teen-agers would buy anything with the word *Beatles* on it. But in England, where people were a bit poorer, a record company might not have been able to get away with short-changing the fans.

No matter how the Beatles' songs were packaged, their records kept selling as fast as ever. People expected sales to drop after Ringo married Liverpool hairdresser Maureen Cox on February 11, 1965. In those days most of the group's fans were still girls, who often dreamed of marrying a Beatle. When she first dated

Ringo, Maureen said, "I had to be careful because of the fans. I might easily have been killed otherwise. Not being married was all part of their image, and none of them were supposed to have steadies."

But if Ringo's female admirers were disappointed, they must have switched their hopes to Paul or George. "Eight Days a Week" went straight to the top of the American hit parade in March, as did "A Ticket to Ride" in May.

More controversial was the June 12 announcement that the queen of England would award the Beatles the MBE. Short for Member of the British Empire, this medal was usually given to powerful businessmen and politicians. Once in a while a writer or a musician might get one for his contribution to the "serious" arts.

By presenting MBEs to the boys from Liverpool, the British government was really thanking them for bringing millions of heavily taxed dollars into the country. As John put it, "If someone had got an award for exporting millions of dollars' worth of machine tools, everyone would have applauded."

Even so, about a dozen of the queen's most distinguished subjects sent back their own medals in a huff as soon as they heard about the Beatles' getting them. Paul Pearson, a former Royal Air Force squadron leader, claimed he did so "because it had become debased." A Canadian politician said he no longer wanted his MBE because it "put him on the same level with vulgar nincompoops." John replied that most of the complainers had earned their medals "for killing people. We received ours for entertaining people. I'd say we deserved ours more. Wouldn't you?"

The queen presented the medals that October, as screaming Beatlemaniacs outside tried to storm her palace gates. The Beatles livened up the solemn occasion with their offbeat sense of humor.

"How long have you been together now?" asked Queen Elizabeth, after she gave Ringo his medal.

"Forty years," deadpanned the drummer.

During the four months between Ringo's wedding and the

MBE announcement, the Beatles had been kept busy working on another movie. Because of the success of the first film, and the group's rise to worldwide fame, United Artists decided to spare no expense in making the second one as exciting as possible.

The movie was shot in color in such far-flung locations as the sunny beaches of the Bahamas and the snow-covered Austrian Alps, where the Beatles had to ski for the first time in their lives—on camera. The single "A Ticket to Ride," says the song is "from the United Artists release *Eight Arms to Hold You*." Everybody thought that's what the movie would be called until, at the last minute, Ringo came up with the title *Help!*

Despite the extra money and effort that went into *Help!*, the film critics did not think it was as good as *A Hard Day's Night*. John, Paul, George, and Ringo had seemed more at home in the settings of the first movie—the concerts, press interviews, and mobs of fans. This time around, they were shown dodging, not screaming girls, but a bloodthirsty Indian cult bent on capturing and killing the bearer of a sacrificial ring—who just happened to be Ringo Starr.

The critics agreed once again that Ringo was the Beatle with the most talent for acting. And *Help!* certainly had its moments as a funny fast-paced comedy that in many ways seemed like a takeoff on the James Bond thrillers, then at the height of their popularity. The problem was that none of it really reflected the Beatles' own lives or personalities. John admitted later that he never liked the movie, saying that director Richard Lester "forgot about who and what we were. It was like having clams in a movie about frogs."

Help!'s music has aged better than the film itself. John still considers the title song to be one of his best and most honest. Though it was used as the theme song for Lester's comedy, on another level it can be heard as a desperate cry for help from a lonely guy who's not as tough as he seems.

The movie also included "I Need You," written and sung by George. The Beatles recorded another Harrison tune, "You Like Me Too Much," around the same time. Though neither of these

The Beatles in one of their many 1965 TV appearances, during which they often just mimed to their records—and didn't even plug in their electric guitars (*Bob Whittaker, Keystone Press Agency*)

Brian Epstein congratulates Ringo and Maureen after their wedding (*Bob Freeman, Transworld Feature Syndicate*)

The Beatles show off their MBEs at a press conference
after receiving the medals from the queen at Buckingham
Palace; Brian Epstein stands at left (*Keystone Press Agency*)

The Beatles with *Help!* leading lady Eleanor Bron (*Popperfoto*)

The Beatles run for second base at New York's Shea
Stadium—where they played to a record-breaking audience
of 56,000 screaming fans (*Keystone Press Agency*)

Cynthia and John Lennon with their son Julian
(*Henry Grossman, Transworld Feature Syndicate*)

ranked among the group's best, they did show that yet a third Beatle was developing a knack for songwriting.

Ringo never managed to write a Beatles song until shortly before the group's breakup, but the others always encouraged him to sing one number on almost every album. The fact that he was a big country-music fan was often shown by the songs he picked. His choice for the *Help!* LP, though not in the film itself, was fitting: "Act Naturally," the story of a homespun fellow who hits the big time in movies by just playing himself.

The most interesting song Paul McCartney wrote for the *Help!* album was "Yesterday." This was a landmark in the Beatles' career for many reasons. For one thing, "Yesterday," with its string quartet was their first recording to use classical instruments. For another, Paul was the only Beatle to actually sing and play on the record. Before long, quite a few of the boys' creations, though still labeled "The Beatles," would only feature one or two members of the group.

But most important, "Yesterday" was a beautiful melody that could appeal to all generations. It was the sort of song that made a lot of older hold-outs decide the Beatles weren't so bad after all. It could also be performed in almost every style by singers and musicians ranging from Ray Charles to Frank Sinatra to Joan Baez. To date, well over a thousand recording artists from almost every country have released their own versions of "Yesterday," making it the most widely interpreted Beatles song ever.

Capitol Records left "Yesterday" and "Act Naturally" off the *Help!* album in America, and they were put out separately on a single instead. "Yesterday" soon became the Beatles' tenth Number One hit song in the United States.

One of John's most popular *Help!* songs was "You've Got to Hide Your Love Away." Strumming simple, repetitious chords on an acoustic (nonelectrified) guitar, he sings with a world-weary twang. It was obvious what had inspired this performance. In a word: Dylan.

The same age as John Lennon, Minnesota-born Bob Dylan had become quite famous on America's college campuses months before "I Want to Hold Your Hand" hit the jackpot for the Fab Four. Accompanying himself back then only with his own acoustic guitar and harmonica, Dylan had made his mark in a scene far removed from the electric beat and hysteria surrounding the Beatles. Most of his fans were young adults who thought rock 'n' roll was cheap and childish. They preferred listening to someone who drew from the "authentic" American folk music that had been around for centuries—and, above all, someone with a message, someone who could put into words the anger and fear they felt about poverty, racial prejudice, and war.

Dylan gave them what they wanted. By 1964 he had stood out from the pack of "folk singers" to become a symbol of the protest movement. Other "folkies" like Peter, Paul, and Mary and Joan Baez became famous largely by doing Dylan's songs. "Blowin' in the Wind" and "The Times They Are a-Changing" provided the soundtrack for marches and demonstrations. The words were powerful and poetic, and far more important than the music—just the opposite of the early Beatles songs.

But, like the Beatles, Dylan had grown up idolizing Elvis Presley and Buddy Holly. And unlike some of his folkie friends, he did not sneer when "I Want to Hold Your Hand" first hit American radio. He liked what he heard.

Despite the difference in their original audiences, the Beatles and Dylan always had one thing in common. This was an almost magical ability to capture, if not create, the mood of the times with their words and music—and even in the way they looked, acted, and dressed. And like the Beatles, Dylan never stayed still. He kept changing and growing, exploring new styles and ideas, at least until the end of the sixties. Wherever the Beatles and Dylan went, everyone else seemed to follow and imitate, trying to keep up with them. In 1965, they began to influence each other.

Just as Dylan admired the Beatles' energetic, electric sound, they were impressed by the honesty and poetry in the songs he sang. They became good friends when he visited them in 1964, turning them on to their first joint at a time when very few people knew about marijuana. But it did not, at first, occur to them to draw from each other's musical ideas. The two styles seemed too different for there to be any common ground.

Then the Byrds came along. Like many other folkies, this group of five Californians had become interested in playing rock 'n' roll after watching *A Hard Day's Night.* They bridged the two worlds once and for all when they recorded Dylan's "Mr. Tambourine Man"—complete with electric guitars, drums, and Beatle-ish harmonies. It became a Number One hit in the summer of 1965.

Dylan himself lost no time in plugging in an electric guitar to record a Number One hit of his own, "Like a Rolling Stone." His words by now had moved away from political topics and toward a more personal "stream-of-consciousness" style. Many of his old fans tried to boo him offstage when he turned up with a rock 'n' roll band, and angrily called him a "sellout."

Meanwhile, countless groups recorded Dylan tunes, or tried to write similar songs of their own. For the rest of 1965, the sound that the press called "Folk-Rock" was the biggest thing on radio. The Beatles—followed by the Rolling Stones, The Who, the Kinks, and all the other groups who had the talent—plus many who didn't—now tried to say something important and interesting with their lyrics. The ones who weren't able to grow and change with the times—like the Dave Clark Five, Gerry and the Pacemakers, and Herman's Hermits—seemed to stop getting hits and were soon forgotten. And the Beatles' next album, *Rubber Soul,* was to have an unmistakable Folk-Rock sound.

But before recording another LP, the Beatles turned America upside-down once again with a late summer tour. This time they only visited ten cities. But because they were now booked only into enormous sports arenas seating tens of thousands of fans, they actually played to about as many people as they had the year before.

The first and most famous show on their 1965 American tour was at New York's Shea Stadium. The audience was the largest for any concert in history up to that time. Fifty-six thousand

Beatlemaniacs packed Shea Stadium to see and hear their idols.

But in fact, all they could really see and hear were the screaming fans in the nearby seats. The stage had been placed behind second base, and unless you had powerful binoculars, the four Beatles seemed no bigger than four insects.

At the best of times, the sound would have been poor. Shea Stadium had been designed for baseball, not music. Also, amplification for rock concerts was primitive by the standards of the 1980s. But the girls in the audience made it difficult to hear a single note. Their screaming completely drowned out the Beatles' voices, and the most anyone could catch was the muddy rumble of guitars and drums.

Few in the audience even knew which songs the Beatles had played until a year later, when a TV film of the event was shown. "Event" is probably the best word to describe a Beatles show from that period, for it was not a concert or a performance in the usual sense when you could hardly hear or see a thing. Rather, it was a celebration of tens of thousands of fanatics sharing in the electricity of each other's enthusiasm, and of the Beatles' mere presence hundreds of feet away.

There were three warm-up acts, which included the miniskirted go-go dancers then considered a basic part of rock 'n' roll. There were also speeches from all of New York's big disc jockeys, who felt they had to be seen at the Beatles concert.

Then John, Paul, George, and Ringo, in matching beige suits, finally leapt on stage. No Concorde jet has ever made as much noise as the audience did at that magic moment. The fifty-six thousand Beatlemaniacs even supplied their own fireworks for the occasion—in the form of Instamatic flashbulbs that kept twinkling, hundreds at a time, throughout the show.

The Beatles opened, as usual, with a short version of "Twist and Shout." Then Paul belted out "She's a Woman," and John took over for "I Feel Fine" and "Dizzy Miss Lizzy." They also sang "A Ticket to Ride," "Can't Buy Me Love," and "Baby's in Black." George got his moment in the spotlight with "Everybody's Trying to Be My Baby," and Ringo with "Act Naturally."

Every few minutes a fan would manage to break through barricades set up to keep back the crowds. He or she would run toward the Beatles until finally dragged away by some of the hundreds of policemen that had been provided by the city of New York. For the next week the newspapers were full of angry letters asking why the taxpayers should have to pay for the Beatles' protection. After all, they made $160,000 for that one concert. As the Beatles never played for more than half an hour in those days, that comes to $100 for each second they stood on stage!

Hundreds of other fans had to be carried out after they fainted from a combination of excitement and New York's sticky August heat. Upon winding up the show with "A Hard Day's Night," "Help!" and "I'm Down," the Beatles fled in an armored car that protected them from fans who couldn't get tickets, but lay in wait outside the stadium anyway.

Each date on the tour brought similar pandemonium—and the kind of money most musicians couldn't hope to earn in years. But the Beatles weren't completely happy with the situation. At a time when they were starting to care more about their words and music, their audiences were neither willing nor able to hear any of it. "How often did we enjoy a show?" asked John. "Once in how many weeks of touring? One show in thirty would give us real satisfaction and you'd go through all kinds of hell for that."

They didn't play in public in the autumn of 1965. They wanted to write and record their new LP at a relatively relaxed pace. The Beatles now had enough money and power to do things their own way. They wanted *Rubber Soul* to be their most brilliant recording yet.

"We finally took over the studio," said John. "In the early days we had to take what we were given; we had to make it in two hours or whatever. On *Rubber Soul* we were more precise about making the album, and we took over the cover and everything."

The cover was indeed unusual for the time. In 1965 rock LP jackets were not expected to show much artistic creativity. The record companies viewed them simply as cardboard containers for a kiddie product, no different from cereal boxes or candy wrappers. Some cute pictures of the smiling stars would be quickly thrown together, with stupid blurbs added for "liner notes." The name of the act was always printed in big block letters.

With *Rubber Soul*, the Beatles began to change all that. For one thing, their name wasn't even on the front cover. This was just about the first time that had been done in America. Of course, nobody needed to be reminded anymore who those four famous faces were.

The picture itself was different from anything people were then used to. The Beatles' faces looked distorted, as if reflected in water, or in the kind of trick mirrors you see at amusement parks. The boys weren't even smiling, and some fans complained that they resembled corpses. All ears but Paul's were now covered by that famous hair. Even the title was a lot more mysterious-sounding than, say, "Beatles '65" or "Something New." It was Paul's pun on "rubber-soled" shoes and "soul" music.

When they recorded *Rubber Soul*, the Beatles were beginning to think in terms of making an album that was not just a collection of different songs that happened to be thrown together on the same record. Though they also made a single at the time, "We Can Work It Out" / "Day Tripper," they persuaded Capitol to release it separately and not include it on the LP. Their American record company had never before put out a Beatles album that did not feature previously released hit singles.

As we mentioned earlier, the songs on *Rubber Soul* show the influence of Bob Dylan and such folk-rock singers as the Byrds. The emphasis is on acoustic guitars and gentle melodies, and— for the first time in the Beatles' career—on the words. But the songs were uniquely their own. Except in "You've Got to Hide Your Love Away" and a few others, the Beatles were never content to simply copy Bob Dylan—or anyone else. Instead, they were inspired by his example to express themselves as creatively and imaginatively as he had—but in their own way.

Many of the songs on *Rubber Soul* and the albums that followed were little stories, complete with distinct characters instead of the usual faceless "she"s, "you"s, and "me"s who were always either happy because they had fallen in love, or sad because they had fallen out of it. "Nowhere Man"—left off the U.S. version of *Rubber Soul* and released later as a single—had nothing to do with romance at all. John's description of his Nowhere Man's empty and aimless life sounds like a real put-down until he adds: "Isn't he a bit like you and me?" We're all Nowhere Men in some way, the Beatles seem to be singing.

"Norwegian Wood," also mainly by John, *was* a love song. But as in Dylan's songs and many that the Beatles themselves would soon write, the words were poetic, mysterious, and hard to understand. John later admitted that he wrote "Norwegian Wood" that way on purpose. He had been seeing another woman, and wanted to describe his love affair without his wife, Cynthia, knowing what he was singing about.

But in late 1965, the strangest and most mysterious thing of all about "Norwegian Wood" was the instrument with which George replaced his usual lead guitar. This was a 21-stringed instrument from India called a sitar.

You can hear a sitar in the instrumental soundtrack to *Help!* where its zingy sound gave some "Eastern" atmosphere to the adventures of that blood-thirsty Indian cult. George was immediately fascinated by the instrument, and bought one for himself. He began listening to India's great sitar player Ravi Shankar, and said that, if he could have one wish granted, it would be to spend the evening inside Ravi's sitar while Shankar was playing a concert. And, of course, George lugged his new toy to the studio while his band was recording "Norwegian Wood."

Soon Indian music would become Harrison's greatest interest in life. And, as always, many other famous musicians began to copy the Beatles. The Rolling Stones, for instance, used a sitar in their next single, "Paint It Black." Donovan, Traffic, Procol Harum, and many others also picked up on the coming "raga-rock" trend. A raga is a form of Indian music, much as a symphony and a concerto are forms of Western classical music.

George's own tunes on *Rubber Soul*—"Think For Yourself" and "If I Needed Someone"—did not show the Indian influence that would soon flavor all his material. But they were a big improvement over his songs on *Help!* and nearly up to the standards of John and Paul's work.

Paul's romantic ballad "Michelle" was almost as successful among the older folks as "Yesterday" had been, though some people found it a bit corny and phony. Far more clever was "Drive My Car," his story about a girl who thinks she's going to become a big star and promises her boyfriend that she'll give him a job driving her limousine after she becomes rich and famous. "Beep-beep, beep-beep, yeah!" sing the Beatles, poking fun at their old "yeah, yeah, yeah" choruses.

Many people thought "In My Life" was the most beautiful song on the album. John sings sadly about all the people and places he used to know that are now gone, but is hopeful that he can build an even better future with the person he loves. For the first time, he wrote the words first as a poem. Then he and Paul set it to haunting music. George Martin added a piano part that sounds as if it could have been written four hundred years earlier. Soon almost every song that the Beatles put out would feature some equally surprising touch.

Rock 'n' roll would never be the same again.

4

New Directions
(1966)

The first Beatle news of 1966 was yet another wedding. Patti Boyd, one of London's most promising models, became Mrs. George Harrison on January 21. The third Beatle wife met George on the set of *A Hard Day's Night*, in which she plays one of the girls who flirt with the Beatles on the train.

Fans seemed to take the news calmly; like their idols, they were also growing up. There were even strong rumors that Paul, too, was about to get married. It was no secret that he was living with Jane Asher, also a beautiful actress and model. Jane had appeared in everything from TV shows and the Michael Caine film *Alfie* to the plays of Shakespeare.

One of mid-sixties London's most glamorous couples, Paul and his red-haired "bird" could often be seen at the openings of plays and art exhibits. They would actually announce their engagement in 1967, but it would be broken off over the following year. Like Patti, Jane added a lot of class to the Beatles' circle.

After George's wedding, the four Beatles stayed pretty much out of the public eye until the early summer. But this was only the calm before the storm. Nineteen sixty-six would prove to be not only their most controversial year, but the one in which the group's music and image—and by extension, that of just about every other rock 'n' roller worth listening to—would change almost beyond recognition. Over the spring the Beatles were holed up writing and recording the songs that would make that possible. Paul described the new music as "sounds that nobody else has done yet—I mean nobody . . . ever!"

The Beatles did emerge from the studios to attend the *New Musical Express* poll-winners' concert on May 1. As in the past, they not only picked up their trophies for being Britain's most popular recording artists, but also gamely played a few songs for the fans. Nobody knew at the time that this would be their last concert in their own country.

Later that month, the first fruits of the quartet's long labors in the studio appeared on a single—Paul's "Paperback Writer" and John's "Rain." Though the Beatles were saving their biggest surprises for the next album, these two songs made even *Rubber Soul* sound ordinary by comparison. At the time, a paperback writer seemed a most unusual subject for a Top Forty hit. Beginning "Dear Sir or Madam," the words to Paul's song take the form of a letter from a struggling writer trying to sell his work to a book publisher. Actually, they probably came very easily to McCartney. Before Brian Epstein came along, Paul, as the Beatles' built-in public-relations man, had often written such letters to promoters in the hopes of getting them interested in his band's music.

"Rain" was the first of many songs in which the Beatles seriously tried to share their philosophy of life with their fans. There is no point, John sings, in letting something like the weather control your mood. Rain and sunshine are all the same to him; he'll make the best of whichever happens to come his way.

"Rain," like "Paperback Writer," is drenched with the electronic effects that the Beatles and George Martin had begun to toy with. Twiddling the recording studio knobs like mad scientists, they distorted their voices and instruments to produce a dreamy, spacy sound. The strangest touch of all turns up at the end of "Rain." John says that after the Beatles recorded the song in one of their all-night sessions, "I got home at about five in the morning . . . staggered up to me tape recorder . . . and just happened to have the tape the wrong way around."

What he heard, much to his amazement, was the Beatles' new song played *backward*. "I was in a trance in the earphones, what *is* it, what *is* it? Too much . . . I really wanted the whole song backwards." So when he got back to the recording studios, he had some of this inside-out music tagged on to the end of the original version—which is why it sounds as if the Beatles are singing "nair" instead of "rain" at the close of the record.

Over the summer of 1966 the group made a world tour that included Germany, Japan, the Philippines, and—after a month's break—North America. All the old symptoms of Beatlemania were still very much in evidence. As ever, the Beatle caravan would hit town like a hurricane, leaving broken barricades, fainting girls, and dazed grown-ups in its wake at each airport, hotel, and stadium. There were all the usual displays of enthusiasm got out of hand. In New York, midtown traffic was tied up for an hour by the spectacle of two girls balanced on a twenty-second-story ledge. They were threatening to jump off unless Paul paid them a visit. Police managed to trick them into thinking their idol was about to arrive—and then took them to a hospital.

Such scenes showed the love, however misplaced, that the fans felt for the group. But on this tour a much nastier reaction also seemed to haunt the Beatles. The summer of 1966 was a season of trouble.

On the last day of their visit to the Philippines, the boys were shown to the airport by a screaming mob out to tear them to pieces—out of hatred. Apparently the wife of the president had expected the Beatles to join her for lunch earlier that afternoon. When her guests didn't appear, it was seen by patriotic Filipinos as a terrible insult to their country. They refused to listen when the musicians explained that they had never even received the First Lady's invitation. Fortunately, the quartet managed to escape intact to India, where John and Paul joined George on a shopping spree for sitars and other Indian instruments.

Meanwhile in America, a big fuss had erupted over an LP cover. Deciding it was time to do something with the material it had held off from the U.S. versions of *Help!* and *Rubber Soul*, Capitol Records had gotten hold as well of three tunes the Beatles had recently taped for their still-unreleased *Revolver*. The company planned to release this grab bag of songs as an LP called *Yesterday and Today*.

The Beatles had helpfully supplied an album jacket, and unbelievably, nobody at Capitol seems to have blinked an eye as 750,000 copies of *Yesterday and Today* tumbled off the presses. For the cover showed the happy mop-tops in a most unusual and gruesome pose: dressed up as butchers and clutching chopped-up baby dolls and hunks of red meat. Could this have been some sort of statement about the way Capitol had been hacking up the Beatles' own "babies"—their record albums—to create more "product" for the marketplace?

But back in 1966, years before Alice Cooper's brand of sick-rock came into style, this sort of stunt was unheard-of—especially on an LP cover. Radio stations who had been sent advance copies filed sharp complaints. Embarrassed Capitol executives quickly figured that in the long run they would lose less money if they substituted another record jacket than if the Beatles' wholesome image went down the drain. The albums were repackaged in 750,000 harmless new jackets, at a huge cost to the company. The surviving "butcher covers" have since become extremely valuable collector's items, worth up to $100 or more in good condition.

That wholesome image, however, was soon in for a far more serious battering—thanks to John Lennon's lifelong habit of saying exactly what he felt without thinking of the consequences. "Everybody takes you up on the words you said," John has complained. "I'm just a guy who people ask about things and I blab off. . . ."

This time he "blabbed off" on the sensitive subject of religion. In an interview with Maureen Cleave of the London *Evening Standard* at the end of 1965, John had expressed the opinion that most young people were more interested in rock 'n' roll than in religion, and that most so-called Christians weren't really following

Jesus' teachings anyway.

"We're more popular than Jesus now," the Beatle had declared. "I don't know which will go first, rock 'n' roll or Christianty. Jesus was all right, but his disciples were thick and ordinary. It's them twisting it that ruins it for me."

Nobody in Britain paid much attention to John's remarks. But when the interview was finally printed in an American teen-age magazine just before the quartet's summer tour, it was quite another story. People thought John was bragging that his group had become more popular than Christ. All across the Bible Belt of the South and the Midwest, God-fearing preachers, politicians, and disc jockeys decided that the time had come to stamp out those creepy Beatles once and for all.

Dozens of radio stations across the South and the Midwest stopped playing Beatle music and began organizing anti-Beatle demonstrations and rallies. Fans were urged to burn their Beatle records and magazines at huge public bonfires. In Birmingham, Alabama, WAQY hired a tree-grinding machine with which to grind its listeners' Beatle albums into dust. Another station put garbage pails on the street outside; printed upon them were the words: "Place Beatle Trash Here."

The rage spread as far as Spain and South Africa, where the Beatles' music would remain banned from the airwaves until 1971. But a few stations *added* Beatle records to their play lists as a way of protesting what they viewed as a dangerous overreaction to John's comments. The Nazis, too, had burned books and records they didn't like. And in London, *Melody Maker* printed an editorial saying that the stupidity of the "reaction to Lennon merely adds weight to his statement that some of Jesus' followers are a bit thick."

When the Beatles arrived in Chicago from England on August 12, John found himself surrounded by microphones and TV cameras. Looking pale and shaky, he tried to apologize without being dishonest. "I suppose if I had said television was more popular than Jesus, I would have gotten away with it. I'm sorry I opened my mouth. I'm not anti-God, anti-Christ, or antireligion.

George and Patti Harrison on
their honeymoon (*Popperfoto*)

Paul and his fiancée, Jane Asher (*Rex Features*)

Throughout America's Bible Belt, Beatles records
and merchandise were hurled into the flames at
rallies protesting John's remark that his group had
become "more popular than Jesus" (*UPI*)

The Beatles leaving London's Heathrow Airport
to begin their last American tour (*Popperfoto*)

John became the first Beatle to make a film without the rest of the band when he took on the role of Private Gripweed in Richard Lester's *How I Won the War*. (*Popperfoto*)

In 1966, George became a follower, student, and close friend of India's sitar genius Ravi Shankar (*Popperfoto*)

I was not saying we are greater or better."

The situation cooled down somewhat, and there were no unpleasant incidents on the tour. The worst that happened was a unanimous vote by the Memphis city council asking the Beatles to cancel their concert there. When they played the Memphis Coliseum anyway, the Ku Klux Klan organized a demonstration outside.

Still, though the audiences and the money and the applause were as big as ever, the Beatles did not consider their concerts a success. They did not enjoy playing them, and felt they were something of a sham. With all that screaming, nobody could or would listen anyway. Yet if people had been able to hear, they might have noticed that the music wasn't very good.

Three years of performing at giant stadiums with dreadful sound systems, to audiences whose own noise made it impossible for them—or the Beatles themselves—to hear the music, had taken their toll. The performers had been reduced to mechanical dolls, going through the motions of being musicians.

In the recording studios, of course, it was another story. But the Beatles were unable to play the material that excited them, that they had just written and recorded for *Revolver*, because of all the electronic effects and additional instruments involved. So, except for "Paperback Writer," they sang mostly the same songs they had the year before—a style of music they felt they had outgrown. They cranked out the old hits halfheartedly, everyone but the always professional McCartney singing off key and tending to forget the words.

Equally fed up with the constant pressures of traveling under strict security measures from one one-night stand to the next, the Beatles made a big decision. They would retire from live performances and pour all their energies into writing and recording. No announcement was made at the time, but the Beatles' concert at San Francisco's Candlestick Park on August 29, 1966, would be the last they ever gave.

The *Revolver* album was released at the beginning of the group's final American visit. Just as that tour marked the end of one Beatle era, so *Revolver* signaled the start of another. *Melody Maker* called it "a brilliant album which underlines once and for all that the Beatles have definitely broken the bounds of what we used to call pop."

When the Beatles first hit the big time, reporters always used to ask them: "When will the bubble burst?" "I figure we're good for another four years," Ringo had said quite truthfully. After all, the careers of rock 'n' roll stars, like other teen-age fads, rarely lasted much longer than that. Elvis Presley was one of the few fifties sensations to have held on to his popularity. But he had done that by turning into a slick "adult" Las Vegas act. Presley certainly hadn't created anything to set the world on its ear since his original string of rock 'n' roll hits in 1955 and 1956.

The Beatles' own brand of wacky, noisy fun had already broken almost every record in show biz. Who else had attracted 56,000 fans to a single performance? Or had had eighteen Number One hits and 20 million sellers within two years in the United States alone?

The Beatles could have left it at that. The fans would have grown up and moved on to other things, the way everyone had originally expected. Beatlemania would have faded to a pleasant memory, leaving behind few lasting effects other than the revolution in men's hairstyles and maybe a few tunes good enough to be watered down and piped over the Muzak machines.

But, as it turned out, the Beatles' music also grew up. The group turned out to be far more brilliant than even their most enthusiastic admirers could have guessed when John, Paul, George, and Ringo first exploded onto the world scene. Less than three years later, their talent for singing and playing, and especially for writing words and music, was beginning to flower into true genius.

What were the ingredients that made *Revolver* so different from what had come before?

The words, for a start. Even more than those on *Rubber Soul*, the Beatles' new songs showed them both exploring their imaginations and observing the world around them. Their writing could be funny, sad, or bitter as it portrayed characters ranging from a pill peddler ("Dr. Robert") to a lonely old spinster ("Eleanor Rigby") to a tax collector ("Taxman").

Then there were the unusual styles of music that the Beatles were now drawing upon to match the subject matter of the words. Touches of Indian, electronic, and classical music had all been added to the palette with which John, Paul, George, Ringo, and producer George Martin had begun to paint their sound pictures.

The Beatles were lucky, of course, to have earned the time and money to experiment in the studios, using professional jazz and symphony musicians as their guinea pigs. They were lucky to have a producer who not only appreciated what they wanted to do, but also had the musical and technical know-how to help them turn their fantasies into reality. And they were lucky to be so famous that people would at least give their strange new sound a hearing. As Paul said, "We're so well established that we can bring our fans with us and stretch the limits of pop." Though earlier records—"Yesterday" with its strings, "Norwegian Wood" with its sitar and weird poetry—had pointed toward new directions, every single song on *Revolver* demonstrated a complete break with the original Beatle sound.

The new music was different in another important sense. Each Beatle was developing as a separate individual, with his own interests and talents—and styles of writing and singing. Though Beatle songs by either John or Paul would always be credited to "Lennon-McCartney," they no longer wrote together except to help each other out when one was feeling stuck. Apart from the background harmonies, the Beatles rarely sang together any longer either. From now on, you could always tell who composed a "Lennon-McCartney" song by who was singing it—(except for "Yellow Submarine," "With a Little Help from My Friends," and "Goodnight," which they wrote for Ringo).

Revolver offered fans a lot of insight into three very brilliant, very distinct personalities. The first to be heard from was George Harrison, who really came into his own on *Revolver* as it featured three of his songs. The album opens with his hard-driving "Taxman."

Brian Epstein once called George "the business Beatle." "He is curious about money," their manager wrote, "and wants to know how much is coming in and what is best to do with it to make it work." So George naturally cast a sharp and angry eye at the British tax system, under which people who earned as much as he did had to pay up to 95 percent. The taxman in Harrison's sarcastic song is, in fact, so greedy that he would even tax the ground the Beatles walk on.

George, however, was feeling generous: he let Paul play lead guitar on "Taxman." McCartney had sometimes been heard to complain that the bass didn't offer enough scope for his musical talents.

"Love You To" showcased George's more recent interest in the sitar. It was his first attempt to write an Indian-style tune, without any Western instruments. Neither John, Paul, nor Ringo appeared on "Love You To"; instead, a gentleman named Anil Bhagwat was brought in to play the tabla, an Indian drum. George, of course, handled the sitar parts himself.

The music of India is very closely tied to Eastern religion, as George had begun to discover. He was reading and learning all he could about Hinduism and Buddhism, and the other Beatles were starting to do the same. These religions strongly warn that money and property tie people down to the material world. To achieve oneness with God, one must transcend, or rise above, such things.

Soon George stopped looking over Brian Epstein's shoulder when their manager was counting the Beatles' earnings. Instead, he led the other three for the first time by getting the group more and more interested in Indian mysticism. He certainly never wrote another Beatle song about money.

Of course, even after the taxman took his fat slice of the pie, George and the others had millions at their disposal—along with worldwide fame, beautiful women, everything that ordinary people spend their lives dreaming about. Yet none of it seemed to make the Beatles feel particularly satisfied. So they began to search for something deeper and more meaningful.

George soon found what he was looking for in Indian religion and culture. It helped him become a much more serene and gentle person, and for a time his enthusiasm captured the other Beatles' interest.

But Eastern mysticism was only one of the dozen ways in which John tried to broaden his horizons and understand the riddle of life. For the rest of his recording career, Lennon would continue to explore many different paths to enlightenment in a restless attempt to come to terms with himself and the world. His ability to share that quest with his listeners was much of what made him a great artist.

By 1966, John's search for answers found him experimenting with LSD and other drugs. Not yet illegal or well-known to the general public, LSD put the user into a dreamlike state that could often turn into a nightmare. Despite the dangers, John, like other young artists of the time, felt that his LSD visions gave him a new outlook and understanding of life. Much of his work on *Revolver* is steeped in the drug experience.

"Dr. Robert" is about John's drug dealer. "She Said She Said" describes an LSD trip Lennon had taken with actor Peter Fonda, who is actually the "she" in the song. "He kept saying in a whisper, 'I know what it's like to be dead,' " Lennon remembered. John's reply: "You're making me feel like I've never been born."

This eerie conversation is set to churning, spaced-out music of the sort that people would soon describe as "psychedelic." That term also fits "I'm Only Sleeping," John's bleary-eyed ode to the joys of staying in bed all day. Here the Beatles repeat the "Rain" gimmick of feeding tapes backward onto the main recording— only this time it is George's guitar that gets that unearthly treatment.

There are many more snippets of backward tapes—usually either speeded up or slowed down, into the bargain—on "Tomorrow Never Knows." This was easily the most psychedelic song of all on the *Revolver* album. The words, which don't even rhyme, were based on *The Book of the Dead,* a Tibetan Buddhist text describing the journey of the soul into the afterlife.

John originally wanted to have a thousand Tibetan monks chanting along, but for once George Martin couldn't fill the order. Instead, each Beatle received the "homework" assignment of creating weird sound effects on their home tape recorders. With an Indian instrument called the tambura droning in the background, Lennon's voice, distorted to sound as if it were blasting out of a faraway foghorn, commanded his listeners to "turn off your mind, relax, and float downstream." It would be a while before most of them understood what he was getting at.

In helping to invent what came to be called "acid-rock" with songs like "She Said" and "Tomorrow Never Knows," John and the Beatles were, as usual, way ahead of their time. But it should be added that, in his ability to explore the LSD experience in his work, John was exceptional. Many artists who relied too heavily on the drug were destroyed by it, or at any rate unable to communicate their ideas to other people. Even John often found his bad trips got the better of him. "I was very paranoid in those days, I could hardly move."

Paul was also learning and exploring. Though he, like all the Beatles, did eventually try LSD more than once, his interests tended to be somewhat more conventional than John's. He took music lessons and checked out classical composers, read widely and dabbled in photography. "I'm trying to cram everything in, all the things that I've missed. People are saying things and painting things and writing things and composing things that are great, and I must know."

Paul's self-improvement campaign helped place his songs on *Revolver* among his best yet. His tunes were growing more sophisticated and varied, ranging from the soul-influenced "Got to Get You into My Life" to the old-fashioned show-tune style of "Good Day Sunshine." On the love songs, "Here There and Everywhere" and, especially, "For No One," Paul's sensitive words did justice to the exquisite melodies.

The most popular of his contributions to *Revolver* was "Eleanor

Rigby," on which John helped out with the words. None of the Beatles plays a note on this number; their place is taken by four violins, two violas, and two cellos.

The saddest Beatle song ever, it laments the loneliness to which so many people's lives are doomed. Eleanor Rigby spends her days by her window, applying makeup from a jar for the benefit of visitors who never arrive. Father McKenzie passes his time writing sermons that "no-one will hear." (Another comment on Christianity's fading influence? People wondered.) The two characters cross paths in the end, when Father McKenzie officiates at Eleanor Rigby's funeral at which nobody shows up. She is "buried along with her name."

"Eleanor Rigby" was one of the songs that helped earn the Beatles the title "spokesmen for their generation." Sociologists and columnists busily analyzed, or tried to read between, every line. They seemed to imagine that understanding the Beatles might provide the key to understanding an entire age group.

A very successful single was released off *Revolver*, pairing "Eleanor Rigby" with "Yellow Submarine." This last was Ringo's showcase, though it was written by John and Paul. "I used to wish I could write songs like the others, and I've tried, but I just can't," Ringo admitted. "Whenever I think of a tune and sing it to the others, they always say 'yeah, it sounds like such-a-thing,' and when they point it out I see what they mean."

"Yellow Submarine" was easily the most off-the-wall song the Beatles had yet done, but it was so irresistibly catchy that for the rest of 1966 you couldn't go anywhere without hearing someone whistling it. Once the Beatles' drug experimentation had become common knowledge, people assumed that the idea of John, Paul, George, and Ringo living a "life of ease" aboard a yellow submarine must have been an LSD brain wave.

Paul denied this. "I knew it would get connotations, but it really was a children's song. I just loved the idea of kids singing it."

The yellow sub was a perfect vehicle for Ringo's goofy, toneless voice. Instrumentally, the song required little more than a few kicks aimed at his bass drum, plus a few simple chords strummed on an acoustic guitar. Since George had no leads, his job was to blow bubbles through a straw. Ocean sound effects were thrown into the mix; and everyone in sight, including engineers and road managers, was dragged before the microphones to chant the "we all live in a yellow submarine" chorus.

Some critics still think *Revolver* is the best album the Beatles ever made. The uncut British version, that is. From now on, however, Capitol would refrain from "butchering" the Beatles' original albums.

In the autumn of 1966, the four Beatles went their separate ways for a few months to pursue individual interests and projects. John—with Ringo tagging along to keep him company— flew to Spain to become the first Beatle to appear in a film without the others. This was an antiwar black comedy called *How I Won the War*, directed by Richard Lester of *A Hard Day's Night* and *Help!* fame. To play the part of Private Gripweed—which he handled well but not outstandingly—John had to crop his hair to a more military length. This made lots of headlines at a time when long hair was still the first thing that came to many people's minds at the mention of the word Beatle. John also stopped wearing contacts and started wearing glasses.

Paul composed the musical score for another movie, *The Family Way*. Then he took off for an African safari.

George went to India for a crash course in the sitar with Ravi Shankar. Cutting his hair almost as short as John's, he also grew a moustache and traveled under a false name so nobody might guess who he was. But, Shankar recalled, "a young Christian page boy happened to recognize him and truly, within 24 hours, almost all Bombay came to know that George Harrison was there. Huge crowds of teen-agers gathered in front of the hotel, headlines appeared in the papers about George's arrival, and my telephone started to ring nonstop. One caller even pretended to be 'Mrs. Shankar.' She changed her mind when I took the telephone myself.

"I could not believe it when I saw this mad frenzy of young

people, mostly girls from twelve to about seventeen. I would have believed it in London or Tokyo or New York—but in India! I couldn't teach and George couldn't practice with all those young people screaming down in the street." Finally, to get some peace and quiet, India's master musician and his star pupil had to leave Bombay for a remote spot near the Himalayan Mountains.

When George returned to England, John, Paul, and Ringo all liked his moustache so much that each began growing one of his own. Then, in November, the four Beatles rejoined forces in a London recording studio to begin work on an album whose impact would amount to a bloodless revolution both in and out of the world of what used to be called pop music.

5

The Summer of Love
(1967)

The year 1966 faded into 1967, and still not a note had been sounded by John, Paul, George, and Ringo since *Revolver*. The silence seemed almost eerie to the fans, who had always been able to count on a new album in time for the Christmas tree. Truly, Beatlemaniacs had been spoiled by the steady flood of releases over the past three years—during which period Capitol Records alone had issued ten different Beatles LPs in the United States. The group's seeming lack of activity began to inspire the first serious rumors of a breakup.

But the Beatles were in fact secluded in the recording studios with George Martin, working harder than ever. Only now they intended to take as much time—and spend as much money—as might be required to produce their all-time masterpiece.

Finally, in February 1967, they released two of their new works on a single. These were John's "Strawberry Fields Forever" and Paul's "Penny Lane"—a "double A-side" if there ever was one.

Both of the new songs' themes reached way back into the boys' past; the single's original sleeve even featured baby snapshots of John, Paul, George, and Ringo. Strawberry Fields was the name of a girls' orphanage in Liverpool that used to host a garden party every summer—to which, as a special treat, Aunt Mimi would bring young John Lennon. Penny Lane is a bustling Liverpool street, full of colorful, friendly characters. Of the song,

Paul said: "It's part fact, part nostalgia for a place which is a great place, blue suburban skies as we remember it, and it's still there."

The Beatles seemed to be taking a last, wistful glance backward with the subject matter of "Penny Lane" and "Strawberry Fields"—even as the recordings themselves showed the group plunging ahead into the unknown. The words and music of the two new songs were more inventive and ambitious than anything they had yet done. "Penny Lane," for instance, was highlighted by some rather complicated trumpet parts. Paul, still unable to write musical notation himself, hummed the tunes to George Martin—who quickly translated what he heard into black dots and squiggles for the benefit of the hired trumpet players.

With their 1967 releases, the Beatles created elaborate audio environments out of sounds and images. Their recordings became stereo fantasy worlds into which listeners might escape again and again, always sure to find some special touch they hadn't noticed before. Paul's wonderfully detailed portrait in words and music made his vision of Penny Lane come to life in the imaginations of millions of people who had never been near Liverpool.

"Strawberry Fields Forever" presents a much stranger picture. "I wrote it about me and I was having a hard time," Lennon later admitted. The song reflects John's experience with LSD, and the trip he takes us on is a lonely, sad, and confused one. We hear him stammering the words as if in a daze, first saying one thing and then the complete opposite, trying in vain to make sense out of his situation. "Nothing is real," John sings; and the only thought he appears able to focus on is a childhood memory of Strawberry Fields.

The real John Lennon must have had his act a bit more together than his self-portrait suggested—for the mysterious music he wrote to describe his confused state of mind ranks with his most brilliant ever. In keeping with the disjointed words, dreamlike cellos suddenly give way to harsh, nightmarish horns. Weird sound effects created by those trusty backward tapes can be heard in the background—along with odd, mumbling voices. Toward the end of the record, the music fades into silence; then, unexpectedly, comes crashing back. An impossibly low voice yawns, "Cranberry sauce"—or is it "I bury Paul"?—and the song is finally over.

"That's John's humor," explained Paul. "John would say something totally out of synch like 'cranberry sauce.' If you don't realize that John's apt to say 'cranberry sauce' when he feels like it, then you start to hear a funny word there and you think 'Aha!' " People were indeed beginning to spend a lot of energy attempting to figure out just what the Beatles were trying to say.

"Strawberry Fields Forever" is a classic example of late-sixties psychedelic music, or "acid-rock." As with many of the Beatles' greatest recordings from this period, much of the final result was arrived at by chance. They had originally taped two versions of "Strawberry Fields"—a slow and a fast one, each in a different key—but felt satisfied with neither. Then George Martin discovered that if the tape of the fast version was slowed down to the speed of the other one, it also would fall into exactly the same key. "Bang," said Paul, "you have the jigsaw puzzle!" What we hear on the record is both versions mixed together. If at times John's voice sounds like a 45 rpm disc being played at 33—well, that's more or less what it is.

To promote the new single—and show the world that the group was still alive and well—the Beatles booked an appearance on "The Ed Sullivan Show." But due to the impossibility of capturing their current sound on their old guitars and drums, they returned to Liverpool to make two short films to accompany the new recordings over the tube.

One depicted the Beatles strolling down Penny Lane, then riding on horseback to a banquet in the middle of a field. The other showed the boys pouring paint over a broken piano before disappearing into the night.

These films seemed as mysterious as the songs themselves, but fans were particularly struck by the way the boys looked. With their moustaches and capes, and John's round rimless spectacles, their "image" had clearly traveled far since their first appearance on "The Ed Sullivan Show."

Like storybook princes, the Beatles were beginning to add a touch of fantasy and wonder to every aspect of their lives—from their brilliantly colored trousers, kaftans, beads, and scarves to their very cars and houses. George had bright rainbows, planets, and stars painted all over the outside of his home in the "stock-broker belt" of London's suburbs. The psychedelic designs on John's Rolls-Royce were so outrageous that a British traffic expert tried to have it banned from the highways. He was convinced that unsuspecting drivers might crash at the very sight of John's controversial car—which today rests peacefully in a New York modern-art museum.

The Beatles had little use for the "straight" nine-to-five types who criticized their unconventional life style. Said George: "Everybody lives their lives thinking 'this is reality' and then say to people like us, 'oh, you're just escaping from reality.' They seriously term this scene of waking up, going out to work, going home again, and all that—reality!"

But the standards, beliefs, and life styles of straight adult society were already under increasing fire in America as well as in Britain. Vietnam was rapidly becoming a focus for young people's discontent. Youths resented being drafted to kill and die in a distant war that their elders generally supported but seemed unable to justify. Many cast a critical eye not only at the government responsible for this nightmare but at the society it represented—and found both wanting. Though America and the rest of the Western world enjoyed the richest standard of living in history, all the cars, color TVs, appliances, and other material comforts hardly seemed to make their owners any wiser, happier, or more tolerant of those who preferred another way of life.

Growing numbers of young people began to reject everything they thought the military, the government, and even their schools and churches stood for. Dropping out of "the system," they created a youth "counterculture" of their own. The more obvious members of this counterculture were tagged "hippies" by the media.

Most of the so-called hippies were under thirty, white, and from well-to-do backgrounds. They could afford to scorn everything their self-made parents believed in—from the flag, the nine-to-five job, and the almighty dollar to the bra, the suit-and-tie, and the crewcut. "Peace" and "Love" were the catchwords of the day. Sharing John Lennon's view that Christianity had become shallow and hypocritical, the counterculture substituted Eastern mysticism, the occult, and astrology for the church. The astrological explanation for the emergence of the counterculture was that the world was entering the new, golden Age of Aquarius.

These idealistic youths considered themselves in the forefront of a revolution that would transform the planet into a magical Utopia. In 1967, anything seemed possible. With their incense, love beads, flowers, and multicolored outfits, the original hippies practically took over such neighborhoods as New York's East Village and San Francisco's Haight-Ashbury, to which all young people were welcomed as brothers and sisters.

Three of the most obvious features of the counterculture were long hair; marijuana and other "mind-bending" drugs (alcohol was out); and the music that was now called, simply, rock. Though the Beatles had never been especially political, much of the counterculture viewed them as heroes and even leaders. The long hair that had become a litmus test of whether a youth was "hip" or "straight" had, of course, been introduced by the boys from Liverpool in 1964. Since then, their appearance, attitudes, and words and music had fallen perfectly in step with the emerging counterculture. Those, for instance, who had taken LSD "high priest" Timothy Leary's famous advice to "turn on, tune in, and drop out" could easily identify with the acid-rock of "Tomorrow Never Knows" and "Strawberry Fields Forever."

But in the spring of 1967, the world at large had yet to put two and two together. The hippie movement still seemed limited to a small cult of weirdos, and much of the media continued to typecast the Fab Four as teen-age heart throbs. Even the boys' own *Beatles Monthly* featured—in extra large print—a letter from a fan who wrote how proud she was that they hadn't got "mixed up in this drugs business. I know if Paul took drugs I'd be worried sick, but I know he's too sensible." The girl was awarded a free subscription for the best letter of the month.

That, oddly enough, was the very month—May 1967—that Paul, the last of the Beatles to try LSD, revealed their secret to two different reporters. "It opened my eyes," he claimed, made him "a better, more honest, more tolerant member of society." Paul later said that he had merely given the journalists a straight answer to the question of whether he had ever tried the controversial drug. *Life* magazine lost little time in trumpeting its hot scoop to millions of subscribers.

The reaction to Paul's remarks on LSD was comparable to that touched off by John's statements about Christianity. Adults shuddered at the thought of millions of young McCartney fans copying their idol's scandalous behavior. The editorial page of England's biggest newspaper, the *Daily Mirror*—which in 1963 had offered such a ringing endorsement of "the nutty, noisy, happy, handsome Beatles"—now denounced their bass player as "an irresponsible idiot."

Everywhere he went, Paul was pestered by reporters and their pointed questions. "It's *you* who've got the responsibility not to spread this," McCartney snapped back. "If you'll shut up about it, I will!" Yet he, the other Beatles, and Brian Epstein soon signed their names to a full-page ad in the London *Times* calling for the legalization of marijuana.

The boys from Liverpool were now openly taking on their role as leaders of the counterculture, which was just starting to catch like wildfire across the Western world. One of the reasons for its dramatic rise was called *Sgt. Pepper's Lonely Hearts Club Band*—the eagerly awaited new Beatles album whose June 1 release ushered in the season of peace demonstrations, free concerts, and outdoor rock festivals that came to be known as 1967's "Summer of Love."

Paul and George in the short film the Beatles made to go with their new single "Penny Lane." Their music was now too complicated for them to even pretend to perform it live *(Keystone Press Agency)*

John's psychedelic Rolls-Royce *(Rex Features)*

Beatles producer George Martin joins Paul at the piano to work out a tune for *Sgt. Pepper's Lonely Hearts Club Band* (*Rex Features*)

The Beatles celebrating the release of their *Sgt. Pepper* masterpiece (*Keystone Press Agency*)

Paul McCartney on the
"Our World" TV special
(*Rex Features*)

The Beatles studying transcendental meditation
with their "guru," the Maharishi Mahesh Yogi
(*Henry Grossman, Transworld Feature Syndicate*)

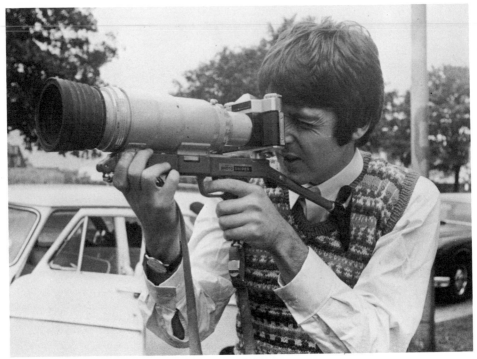

The *Magical Mystery Tour* film was a Paul McCartney
brainwave—and the Beatles' first flop (*Popperfoto*)

John on the *Mystery Tour* bus
(*Keystone Press Agency*)

George in one of his *Magical
Mystery* outfits (*Popperfoto*)

At the time, almost everything about this record seemed revolutionary and astonishingly brilliant. Even the double fold LP jacket was the most elaborate the rock-music world had ever seen. For the photograph on the front cover, the group had specially built a twelve-foot-square garden. Over loose dirt suggesting a freshly dug grave (*Whose?* people wondered), they planted flowers to form the shape of a guitar and the letters of the word "Beatles." Knickknacks and statues from their own personal collections were strewn among potted palms and marijuana plants.

In the background was assembled a crowd of sixty-two lifesize cardboard cutouts of the Beatles' favorite historical, literary, and show-biz characters. These included Einstein, Lewis Carroll, Edgar Allan Poe, and Marilyn Monroe. The Beatles and their assistants had had to go to great lengths to find pictures of each one, blow them up to the right size, and obtain legal permission from those personalities—such as Bob Dylan, Shirley Temple, and Marlon Brando—who were still living.

A top London theatrical agency was brought in to tailor bright satin Lonely Hearts Club Band uniforms for the Beatles themselves to pose in. Clutching trumpets, John, Paul, George, and Ringo were now ready to take their place center stage in their fantastic new show.

(Brian Epstein, by the way, thought the Beatles were going too far with all this. Before boarding a flight in the spring of 1967, he scrawled the words "brown paper bags for Sgt. Pepper" as his last wish in case the plane crashed.)

The album also contained a sheet of cardboard souvenirs. And, so that listeners would be sure to pay attention to the all-important words of their new songs, the Beatles insisted that they all be printed on the back cover. This had never been done before on a major rock release; since then, like so much that the Beatles introduced, it has become commonplace.

The record itself boasted more musical variety than any other Beatles LP. *Sgt. Pepper* was a crazy quilt of rock 'n' roll and classical, folk, Indian, vaudeville, and electronic influences. Yet it all hung together to give the effect of a continuous show, or "magic presentation" as Paul called it. This was in part because the Beatles (again for the first time on a rock LP) did away with the few seconds of silence separating one song from the next. As in a dream—or, some imagined, an acid trip—anything was likely to happen next—and the more unexpected, the better.

The first sounds we hear on *Sgt. Pepper* are the hum of a restless audience and an orchestra tuning up its instruments. Then the actual show begins with the theme song. Paul's "Sgt. Pepper's Lonely Hearts Club Band" starts out as the closest thing to rock 'n' roll on the whole album—but McCartney's message is all old-fashioned show-biz charm: *Sit back and let the evening go. . . .* Strange things, however, soon happen to the music. The trumpet parts, for instance, sound as if they might have been written three hundred years earlier.

To cheers from the invisible crowd, Ringo—introduced as Billy Shears—takes the spotlight for "With a Little Help From My Friends." Playing his role of the bumbling clown to the hilt, he admits he has trouble singing in tune, but begs us all to bear with him. With a little help from his friends, he'll get by—and "get high."

A lot of people caught a whiff of pot in that last turn of phrase. In 1970, Vice-President Spiro Agnew would unsuccessfully campaign to have the song banned from American radio. But John insisted it was "really a sincere message" about the importance of friendship. "With a Little Help" certainly summed up the personality of the warm and easygoing Ringo, who had the smallest ego of all the Beatles, and who most needed the support of his three talented friends.

The likes of Spiro Agnew were even more upset by the next song on the album. Not only were the words suspiciously imaginative—but the first letters in the title "Lucy in the Sky with Diamonds" actually spelt out those wicked initials LSD.

That, John claims, was pure coincidence. The title was originally dreamed up by his son, four-year-old Julian Lennon, for one of his own drawings. In any case, John's "rocking-horse people with marshmallow pies" may well owe more to his lifelong love of Lewis Carroll than to any drug. Said Paul: "We did the whole thing like an *Alice in Wonderland* idea, being in a boat on the river, slowly drifting downstream with those great *cellophane flowers towering over your head*. Every so often it broke off and you saw Lucy with Diamonds all over the sky." Still, much of the counterculture viewed the song in the same light as Agnew—and were as delighted as he was not.

Paul's "She's Leaving Home" also seemed to sum up a common counterculture experience. Hippie neighborhoods such as Haight-Ashbury swarmed with young runaways. Like the girl in the Beatles' song, most had left middle-class homes and parents who'd struggled to give them "everything money could buy." "She's Leaving Home" 's semiclassical music reminded people of "Eleanor Rigby," though the new song was actually far more complicated. The tricky counterpoint on the chorus between the voices of John, Paul, and George provides just one example of "She's Leaving Home" 's musical brilliance. But the words have been criticized as being little more than a corny tearjerker.

Sgt. Pepper's Lonely Hearts Club Band seldom loses its carnival atmosphere—which becomes the actual subject of "Being for the Benefit of Mr. Kite." McCartney explained where Lennon got not only the title but also many of the words: "John has this old poster which says right at the top 'Pablo Fanques Fair Presents the Hendersons for the Benefit of Mr. Kite,' and it has all the bits of things that sound strange: *Over men and horses, hoops and garters, lastly through a hogshead of real fire.*"

"Mr. Kite" offers a good example of the unconventional methods the Beatles used not only in writing but also in recording their 1967 songs. George Martin recalls some of the lengths he went to in getting the "carnival sound" John wanted: "I got dozens of old steam organ tapes. I cut the tapes into 15-inch lengths and told the engineer to throw them all up and stick them back together again, which he did. We had a tape which had no musical shape and which was nonsense. But it *was* the sound of a steam organ, and created a floating, fairground sound. And that's how 'Mr. Kite' was done. Like a huge jigsaw puzzle."

Side two opens with "Within You Without You," a George Harrison raga-rock sermon featuring a large group of Indian musicians. In one of *Sgt. Pepper*'s most startling sleights of hand, the hippie-style "Eastern mysticism" suddenly gives way to the 1920's sounds of "When I'm 64." This was Paul's salute to the older generation—particularly his father, Jim, who had just turned sixty-four. "When I'm 64" (like "Lovely Rita," which comes next) shows just how witty Paul's words could be when he made the effort.

John's "Good Morning Good Morning" takes aim at the empty greetings people use to hide the fact that they actually have nothing to say to each other. By the end of the song, language has been replaced by meaningless animal noises. In a recording trick for which George Martin has received many compliments, the last "note" of "Good Morning," the clucking of a chicken, turns into the sound of a guitar. "Sgt. Pepper's Lonely Hearts Club Band" returns for a second version, to say thank you and good night.

But the band lingers on for one encore, which many people consider *the* masterpiece not only of the *Sgt. Pepper* LP but also of the group's entire career. "A Day in the Life" actually started out as two songs John and Paul had been working on separately. Both Beatles got bogged down—until it occurred to them to stick the two unfinished pieces together, and the puzzle fell into place.

"A Day in the Life" opens with John's eerie account of a fatal car crash. A crowd gathers round, wondering if the victim is someone they recognize from the newspapers. Then John describes another crowd, at the showing of his antiwar film *How I Won the War*. To an audience unwilling or unable to understand, Lennon addresses "A Day in the Life" 's key words: "I'd love to turn you on." At this the forty-one instruments of London's Royal Philharmonic Orchestra launch into an extraordinary passage that reminded some listeners of the initial "rush" caused by certain drugs.

The mad orchestra is suddenly switched off, and replaced by the everyday sound of a single piano. An alarm clock rings, as if to indicate that the first part of the song had been someone's dream. "The next bit," said Paul, "was just me remembering what it was like to get up, run up the road to catch a bus to school, having a smoke and going into class." But McCartney only gets as far as his smoke, which sends him—and the music—back "into a dream."

From here on, there is no returning to the dull world of reality. Lennon babbles like a lunatic about filling a London concert hall with "holes." After an even more powerful rush from the Philharmonic Orchestra, the Beatles' "Day in the Life" finally ends with a single doom-filled chord that lasts nearly a minute.

Because of its supposed "drug references," "A Day in the Life" became the first Beatles song to be banned by the BBC, which held a monopoly over British radio. Paul admitted that "this was the only one on the album written as a deliberate stick-that-in-your-pipe." But he added: "What we want is to turn you on to the truth, rather than pot."

Sgt. Pepper's Lonely Hearts Club Band won high praise from nearly everyone who wrote about it—including such classical composers as Ned Rorem and Leonard Bernstein. The critic for New York's *Village Voice* called it "the most successful and most ambitious record album ever issued."

But *Sgt. Pepper* was much more than an exceptionally brilliant LP. As far as the counterculture was concerned, the boys from Liverpool had said it all. The generation gap, the drug experience, the fascination with fantasy and magic and Eastern mysticism—all seemed to be summed up within the grooves of the Beatles' new album. *Sgt. Pepper* quickly spread the word on the new youth life styles to millions of people who had not already "turned on, tuned in, and dropped out."

As the counterculture's first certified work of art, *Sgt. Pepper* also inspired people to begin writing seriously about rock music for the first time. Dozens of new publications, such as *Rolling Stone*, sprang up in 1967 to provide an outlet for rock journalism and criticism.

With *Sgt. Pepper*, the music world itself changed almost beyond recognition. Old standards of what was or wasn't "commercial" seemed to go right out the window. The counterculture encouraged extremes of individuality and nonconformity—even weirdness—and popular music stars were now expected to embody these qualities.

Rock enjoyed a period of almost total freedom of expression. Songs on albums—previously limited to about three minutes—could now run to thirty seconds or half an hour. Any topic, any style of music, were fair game.

New, electronically-minded groups such as Pink Floyd began to make a mark on London's "underground" scene with bizarre songs about magic and space travel. In America, such hippie bands as the Grateful Dead and Jefferson Airplane broke out of San Francisco's Haight-Ashbury to acquire a national following. With their psychedelic light shows and other special effects, these bands turned each of their performances into a dazzling spectacle for the eye as well as the ear.

Of course, much of the new music was hardly up to the level of the Beatles'. Just as groups like the Dave Clark Five had cashed in on the Fab Four's original style and image, now there were hundreds of imitation *Sgt. Peppers* to contend with. Stringy-haired also-rans, such as Strawberry Alarm Clock, the Seeds, and the Vanilla Fudge, dished up enough nonsense words, pointless sound effects, and tuneless junk to keep record factories busy for months.

One quality that set the Beatles apart from even the best of these new bands is that the boys from Liverpool almost always kept their songs highly tuneful—and short and sweet. Unlike other ego-tripping music stars, John, Paul, George, and Ringo never launched into the endless guitar or drum solos that were becoming so commonplace. Each Beatle limited his contribution to whatever might make the song itself come across as appealingly as possible.

Sgt. Pepper also inspired established groups such as the Rolling Stones and The Who. The Stones tried to make their next album, *Their Satanic Majesties Request,* even more psychedelic than the

Beatles'—to the point of creating a three-dimensional LP cover depicting the quintet in a spaced-out fantasy land. But *Satanic Majesties* was harshly criticized as a *Sgt. Pepper* rip-off, and the Stones quickly got back to playing rock 'n' roll.

The Who took the idea of a "concept album" a step further than the Beatles had. They began recording their double-album *Tommy*, in which all the songs related to a complicated story about a deaf, dumb, and blind boy's search for the truth.

The next release by the Beatles themselves was another single. While working on *Sgt. Pepper*, they had accepted an invitation to represent Britain on a very special TV program called "Our World." The June 25 show was to be broadcast live by satellite to at least 150,000,000 viewers in almost every country.

The Beatles were asked to write and perform a special new song, with words simple enough to be understood by people who might know very little English. Following these instructions, John came up with "All You Need Is Love." The Beatles decided it was good enough to be their next single, with "Baby You're a Rich Man," also by John, as the B side.

"All You Need Is Love" perfectly fitted not only the spirit of international brotherhood projected by the TV program but also the spirit of the counterculture's own "Summer of Love." Yet at the same time, the new single—which even includes a sarcastic chorus from "She Loves You"—was something of a satire of the so-called Love Generation that the Beatles were supposed to be leading. The song showed that the boys were not taking their new role *too* seriously.

On August 8—after a stay on Hollywood's Blue Jay Way, which he captured in song on the spot—George Harrison personally checked out the Haight-Ashbury scene. Sporting a pair of heart-shaped purple sunglasses, the Pied Piper from Liverpool attracted a large, adoring train of flower children as he wandered down the "Hashbury" streets, strumming a guitar and singing "Baby You're a Rich Man."

But George had already left the hippie drug scene behind him. "A hippie," he said, "is supposed to be someone who becomes aware; you're hip if you know what's going on. But if you're really hip you don't get involved with LSD and things like that. It can help you to go from A to B, but when you get to B, you see C. And you see that to get really high, you have to go at it straight. There are special ways of getting high without drugs—with yoga, meditation, and all those things."

For some time, George had been searching for an Indian guru, or spiritual master, who could teach him about "all those things." Finally he met the Maharishi Mahesh Yogi, whose brand of Transcendental Meditation—TM for short—seemed almost unbelievably easy and effective. TM did away with the complicated ritual of most Hindu cults. All that the Maharishi's followers had to do was to silently repeat a magic word—or mantra—to themselves for twenty minutes twice a day. Many meditators claimed that doing this had made them happier, healthier, more loving and creative human beings. High on their mantras, they no longer needed alcohol or drugs.

All four Beatles were quickly sold on TM. Like other restless young Westerners, they wanted to discover the "answers" Eastern religions seemed to offer—without having to undergo the severe spiritual discipline most cults demanded. The Beatles connection gave the little-known Maharishi all the publicity he had ever dreamed of. TM became all the rage, not only in the counterculture, but eventually among straight businessmen and housewives as well. United States General Franklin Davis and Apollo 11 astronaut Michael Collins were among the millions who would learn to overcome stress with a mantra. Like so much we take for granted today, this might not have happened were it not for the Beatles. Suddenly, there was a new fifth Beatle as far as the press was concerned: a tiny, scraggly-haired old Hindu monk who seemed to suffer from constant fits of the giggles, even when he was lecturing on the meaning of life.

John, Paul, George, and Ringo all agreed to attend an August weekend meeting of the Maharishi's followers in Bangor, Wales. The press, as usual, turned the expedition into a circus. Mobs of reporters, photographers, and fans showed up to watch the Beatles board their train to Bangor.

Whatever peace and contentment they found in the course of the weekend was rudely shattered by tragic news. Brian Epstein had died from an overdose of sleeping pills on August 27, at the age of thirty-two.

"I was scared," remembered John. "I thought, we've had it. He had great qualities and he was good fun. He had a flair. He was a theatrical man, rather than a businessman. We'd never have made it without him, and *vice versa*. Brian contributed as much as us in the early days, although we were the talent and he was the hustler."

Brian Epstein, never a happy man, had felt increasingly at loose ends over the past year. The Beatles' retirement from concert performances had left him with little to do on their behalf. He had begun to wonder whether his boys even needed him any more. But over the months following his death, the Beatles would find themselves making some foolish moves that Brian would certainly have warned them against.

They didn't, at first, try to find a new manager. "No one could possibly replace Brian," said Paul, who himself took over the job of holding the group together, keeping an eye on their finances and guiding their career. According to John, "Paul made an attempt to carry on as if Brian hadn't died by saying, 'Now, now, boys, we're going to make a record.' And that's when we made *Magical Mystery Tour*."

This was to be an hour-long TV film, written and directed by the Beatles themselves. The Beatles' press releases offered this sketch of the plot: "Away in the sky, beyond the clouds, live four or five magicians. By casting Wonderful Spells they turn the Most Ordinary Coach Trip into a Magical Mystery Tour...."

The "Mystery Tour" was largely Paul's trip. He felt that the Beatles needed something to keep them in the public eye in the absence of concert tours. The best solution seemed to be what John called "a film vehicle to go with the new music." They would attempt to duplicate in a movie all the fantasy, wonder, and strangeness of their recent records. But while they were now seasoned professionals in the recording studio, the Beatles—as Paul himself admitted—"didn't know anything about making films."

Nonetheless, they rented a bus, painted it bright colors, filled it with a cast of oddballs, and bombed merrily about the English countryside. Sometimes the Beatles staged scenes they had written themselves in advance, but mostly they just filmed whatever happened to happen. The result was a colorful home movie, full of gimmicks—such as slow and fast motion, double exposures and dizzy zooms in and out of close-up—that bring to mind clever kids playing with a new toy. Despite some nice shots of the Beatles in wizards' outfits and white tuxedoes, even devoted fans often found *Magical Mystery Tour* more tiresome than mysterious when it was shown to fifteen million Britons on December 26.

England's newspapers pounced like jackals. The TV film appeared to be the first flop of the Beatles' professional career, and the press played the story to the hilt. "The harder they come, the harder they fall," proclaimed a front-page review in London's *Daily Express*. "I cannot ever remember seeing such blatant rubbish."

Paul tried to put a good face on its failure, saying: "I think it was a good show. It will have its day, you know." But plans to air *Magical Mystery Tour* in the United States were scrapped, though it has since turned up as a midnight screening at youth-oriented cinemas.

Magical Mystery Tour's music, unsurprisingly, was far more popular than the film itself. Very much in the style of *Sgt. Pepper*, the new songs did include several rehashes of the last album. But Paul's beautiful ballad "Fool on the Hill" and, especially, John's "I am the Walrus" were two of the most fascinating and original Beatles songs ever.

Much of "I am the Walrus" could—like "Lucy in the Sky"—be traced to John's obsession with Lewis Carroll's work—particularly the poem in *Through the Looking-Glass* that begins " 'The time has come,' the Walrus said, / 'To talk of many things: / Of shoes—and ships—and sealing-wax / Of cabbages and kings. . . .' " Over the years, said John, the Walrus "became symbolic of me."

In "I am the Walrus" Lennon takes the art of Lewis Carroll-style nonsense about as far as it can be taken by a song. "Walrus" features some of his most marvelous and outrageous images, but even John admitted he hadn't a clue as to what the whole thing was supposed to mean.

The music itself was inspired by the sound of an approaching police siren. The unnerving repetition of the siren's two notes propels John's "Walrus" toward the brink of total insanity with its robotlike beat. Those mad geniuses of the recording studio, the Beatles and George Martin, pile on the layers of cellos, violins, horns, and, finally, a boys' choir chanting "oompah, oompah, stick it up your jumpah." We hear crackling voices drift in and out of the music, as if somebody were fiddling with the dial of a radio. But when the music fades at last, the voices continue; and we find we've been listening to a reading of part of Shakespeare's *King Lear*. Thus ends acid-rock's finest moment.

In England, the six *Magical Mystery Tour* numbers were put out in a highly unusual package containing two seven-inch EP records and a twenty-four-page picture book. But for the American market, Capitol stretched out the record (and book) to the usual twelve-inch LP size—by adding all the songs the Beatles had released as singles over the previous year.

Apart from *Magical Mystery Tour*, the biggest Beatles' headlines at the end of 1967 concerned, of all things, a clothing shop. The boys from Liverpool had decided to invest some of their fortune in a boutique they named Apple, which Paul described as "a beautiful place where you could buy beautiful things." A team of Dutch hippies called simply "the Fool" were hired to give the outside of the building the same otherworldly look they had splashed all over George's suburban home. Other businesses on London's Baker Street sued in vain to have Apple's bright rainbows, planets, clouds, and mystical symbols blotted out with a more respectable shade of paint.

The Fool also designed much of the expensive merchandise offered at Apple. This included the likes of tangerine-colored velvet capes, and costumes created from Indian cloth and Greek beads to represent "Fire," "Water," or "Space." On the much sought-after invitations to sip apple juice with the stars at the December 5 opening, even the schedule seemed magical and mysterious: "Come at 7:46. Fashion show at 8:16." (The only Beatles to turn up were John and George. Paul was fixing up his new farm retreat in Scotland; and Ringo was off to Rome, starring in his first non-Beatle film, *Candy*.)

But the Beatles soon grew bored with their boutique. "We decided the retail business wasn't our particular scene," said Paul. One morning, eight months later, startled customers were told they could keep their money—and the merchandise of their choice as well. News of the giveaway quickly spread; and by the time the press got wind of it, the mob scene on Baker Street had turned into a virtual riot. By the end of the day, Apple had been completely cleared of $25,000 worth of clothing, and the shop was shut down for good.

According to John, it was he who "came up with the idea to give it all away and stop screwing around with a psychedelic clothes shop. So we gave it all away. It was a good happening."

The name Apple, however, would soon turn up on an even more starry-eyed vision.

6

Blue Meanies in Pepperland
(1968)

The new year found the Beatles as high on meditation as ever. The whole group signed up for a three-month advanced TM course at the Maharishi's retreat in the Himalayan Mountains.

Before their February 21 departure, they recorded several new numbers. Two of these—John's "Across the Universe" and George's "The Inner Light"—described the effects of meditation. But a plan to release both songs on a single while the Beatles were off with the Maharishi fell through. John rated "Across the Universe" among his most beautiful songs—"It's one of the best, it's good poetry," he said—but he felt dissatisfied with the way it actually turned out in the studio. The recording was donated to a British charity LP aiding the World Wildlife Fund, and Paul's "Lady Madonna" wound up as the A side of the single.

There was nothing mystical or even psychedelic about "Madonna," the first Beatles recording in years to explore their original rock 'n' roll roots. "It sounds like Elvis, doesn't it?" said Ringo. "No, it doesn't sound like Elvis. It *is* Elvis."

"The Inner Light" was the first Harrison song to make it onto a Beatles single. Perhaps the best of George's raga-rock efforts, the background instruments had been taped on one of his earlier trips to India. "Forget the Indian music and listen to the melody," said Paul. "Don't you think it's a beautiful melody? It's really lovely."

The words also seemed impressive—until a sharp-eyed fan unearthed an old Japanese poem, some of which read: "Without going out of his door, he knows everything in the world. Without looking out of his window, he knows the way to heaven." That, almost word for word, is what George sings in "The Inner Light." Despite his holy image, he wasn't above pinching from other people's work now and then. One day this habit would get him into trouble.

Disillusionment began to set in soon after the Beatles arrived in India. After only ten days at the Maharishi's retreat, Ringo was back in London, complaining that the place reminded him of Butlin's (a British holiday camp for working-class kids). Also, he said, "The food was too spicy."

A few weeks later, Paul left as well. John and George almost saw the course through—until they heard rumors that the Maharishi had been making passes at their fellow meditator Mia Farrow. John was infuriated by what he viewed as the monk's hypocrisy, and talked George into coming home with him. John even wrote a new song called "Maharishi." In it he attacked his guru, "the latest and the greatest of them all," for having "made a fool of everyone." But when Lennon's anger cooled off, he changed the Maharishi's name—and gender—to "Sexy Sadie." "I was a bit rough to him," John later admitted. "I always expect too much."

The trip to India—the last the four Beatles would ever take together—ended in a shambles; but they accomplished a great deal while they were there. Thanks to the magic powers of meditation—or, perhaps, the lack of anything to distract them—John, Paul, and George composed no fewer than thirty new songs at the Maharishi's retreat. Even Ringo managed to write a tune (country style, of course), called "Don't Pass Me By," his first ever.

Now that they were all back in England, the Beatles began mapping out the most ambitious scheme of their entire career. Still under the spell of the "Spirit of Sixty-Seven," they decided to use their immense wealth and reputation to create their own company. This would be the first multimillion-dollar, multi-media corporation to be run both by and for the so-called Now Generation, without any interference from the "men in suits." The boys from Liverpool named the company Apple Corps. ("That's a pun," said Paul helpfully.)

They worked out a deal with their record company enabling them to put out all new Beatle releases on their own Apple Records. (Capitol would distribute these in America, and EMI elsewhere.) They also intended to set up an entire network of related businesses, such as Apple Electronics, Apple Books, and Apple Films.

John and Paul flew to New York to announce their grandiose plans at a floating press conference on a Chinese junk, and over the Johnny Carson show to Joe Garagiola and some ten million TV viewers. Said Paul: "We always had to go to the big man on our knees, touch our forelocks, and say, 'Please, can we do so and so?' And most of those companies are so big, and so out of touch with people like us who just want to sing and make films, that everybody has a bad time. We're just trying to set up a good organization, not some great fat institution that doesn't care. If you come to see me and say 'I've had such-and-such a dream,' I will say 'Here's so much money. Go away and do it.' "

As if that wasn't enough to put stars in the eyes of every struggling artist on the planet, the Beatles even placed a full-page want ad in the British music papers. Printed below a photograph of a young musician were the words "THIS MAN HAS TALENT. One day he sang his songs to a tape recorder, and, remembering to enclose a picture of himself, sent the tape to Apple Music, 94 Baker St., London W.1. If you were thinking of doing the same thing yourself, do it now! This man now owns a Bentley!"

To nobody's surprise—except, it seems, the Beatles'—Apple was immediately swamped with tapes, manuscripts, and nutty proposals, many of which were delivered in person. "All the lepers in Britain and America came to see us," said John. "Our lives were getting insane! I tried to see everyone like we said, everyone day in and day out, and there wasn't anyone who had anything to offer to society or me or anything. There was just 'I want, I want, and why not?' and terrible scenes in the offices with different spades and hippies, all very wild with me. We had to quickly build up another wall round us to protect us."

But both Paul and George did discover a number of talented unknowns. These included James Taylor, Billy Preston, Mary Hopkin, and Badfinger, all of whom received their first taste of stardom through Apple Records.

A Greek friend of John's named Magic Alex was put in charge of Apple Electronics. This self-styled mad genius spent thousands of dollars of the Beatles' money on creating such items as fruit-shaped radios and a "nothing box" guaranteed to do absolutely nothing for five years. But none of Magic Alex's inventions ever made it to the marketplace.

Despite those heaps of unsolicited manuscripts, tapes, and films left to gather dust, Apple Corps generally lived up to its original spirit for the next year or so. Few business decisions were made without first consulting an astrologer. Liquor—and other intoxicants—flowed freely throughout business hours. Groups of hippies, Hell's Angels, and nudists moved into Apple's Savile Row offices and quite literally made themselves at home. Nobody wanted to seem "unhip" by asking them to leave.

Apple was officially launched in August 1968, with the release of four singles, including the Beatles' own "Hey Jude" / "Revolution." All featured an eye-catching label design—a whole green apple on the A side, a sliced apple for the B side. The new record company proclaimed August 11 through 18 "National Apple Week," and delivered gift presentation boxes of "Our First Four" to the palaces of Queen Elizabeth, the Queen Mother and Princess Margaret, and to the Prime Minister's residence at 10 Downing Street. The sixty-eight-year-old Queen Mother wrote a thank-you note saying she was "greatly touched by this kind thought from the Beatles" and "much enjoyed listening to these recordings."

Apple Records could scarcely have gotten off to a more brilliant start. In America, Paul's "Hey Jude" turned out to be the biggest-selling single the Beatles ever released. Another of Apple's "First Four"—McCartney discovery Mary Hopkin's "Those Were the Days"—followed it to the top of the charts on both sides of the Atlantic.

"Hey Jude" opens to the lonely sound of Paul's voice and piano. Other instruments and voices are gradually added. By the time the record explodes into its endless chanted fade-out, we hear a forty-piece symphony orchestra as well. "We decided to make double use of the forty musicians," said Beatles assistant Mal Evans, "by asking them if they'd like to do a bit of singing and clap their hands. They were quite pleased to oblige."

The song was originally called "Hey Jules." Paul began it as a musical pep talk for five-year-old Julian Lennon, whose parents' marriage—as the world would soon see—was on the rocks.

"Hey Jude" was the longest 45 rpm record the Beatles—or anyone else—had ever released. Top Forty radio stations hated to include singles much over three minutes long on their tight play lists. But the Beatles were so popular—and their new song so good—that disc jockeys had no choice but to air it. "Hey Jude" clocked in at an unheard-of—yet evidently lucky—seven minutes and eleven seconds.

The sliced-apple side of the record was also extremely popular—and controversial. The high-energy rock music of John's "Revolution" packed the punch of a heavyweight champion— but it was the words that the counterculture's political radicals took as a slug in the face, if not a stab in the back. Though most longhairs were still sold on peace and love, a loud minority favored a violent revolution as the only way to change society. "Revolution" was John's response to this argument.

"The idea," he said later, "was don't aggravate the pig by waving the red flag in his face. You know, I really thought that love would save us all. There were two versions of that song, but the underground left only picked up on the one that said 'Count me out.' The version on the LP says 'Count me in' too; I put both in because I wasn't sure. On the single I said: *When you talk about de-*

struction you can count me out. I didn't want to get killed."

Along with the launching of Apple Records, the Beatles' summer of '68 was highlighted by the release of their feature-length animated movie *Yellow Submarine.* The real-life Beatles had in fact had little to do with this project, apart from their brief appearance at the film's end and their contribution of four unused *Magical Mystery Tour*-era recordings to the sound track. Even the voices of *Yellow Submarine*'s John, Paul, George, and Ringo characters were actually those of professional actors. Paul himself admitted: "I like what I've seen about it, but it's not us. I won't take the credit even if it's a big smash."

Nonetheless, the plot of this highly imaginative psychedelic cartoon was based on the Beatles' own songs—and *Yellow Submarine* managed to capture their spirit of fantasy and wonder far more successfully than *Magical Mystery Tour* had. According to *Yellow Submarine*'s producer Al Brodax, the project was originally inspired by a three A.M. telephone call from John Lennon, who asked him: "Wouldn't it be great if Ringo was followed down the street by a yellow submarine?"

"We derived a lot from the *Sgt. Pepper* album," said Brodax. "We took the word 'pepper' which is positive and spicy, and created a place called Pepperland which is full of color and music. But in the hills around live Blue Meanies, who hate color, hate everything positive."

German poster-artist Heinz Edelmann used five million separate sketches in piecing together the animated movie. The artwork included a dazzling array of styles, ranging from Walt Disney to surrealism to Art Nouveau. *Yellow Submarine* was certainly one of the most lavish feasts for the eye ever to be placed on film. Like Disney's *Fantasia,* it worked best when set to music. Many film critics found that the silliness of the dialogue quickly grew tiresome, but most gave *Yellow Submarine* rave reviews on the strength of the stunning visuals—and the Beatles' songs.

Yellow Submarine set off the second tidal wave of Beatles trinkets. The list of seventy-five licensed items included dolls, stationery, lunch boxes, and even a yellow-submarine Corgi toy,

Paul and John leave for New York
to announce their formation
of Apple Corps—the counterculture's first multimillion
dollar corporation (*Popperfoto*)

The Beatles rehearsing for their
brief, real-life appearance at
the end of *Yellow Submarine*
(*Transworld Feature Syndicate*)

John—seen at his London exhibit of White Art—found in Yoko Ono a new partner in both his love life and his creative work (*Popperfoto*)

The real-life Blue Meanies struck back at the outrageous couple with a marijuana arrest (*UPI*)

complete with revolving periscopes and hatches from which little plastic Beatles popped up at the flick of a switch. Like the film itself, this merchandise updated the Fab Four mop-top image of the 1964 novelties to fit the psychedelic styles of the late sixties. It also showed how quickly "the system" had managed to turn the counterculture into a highly profitable business. As one film reviewer put it: "Attacks on the consumer society become products to be consumed."

All four Beatles attended *Yellow Submarine*'s July 17 London premiere. The wild scene outside the theater recalled the Beatlemania of days gone by; this, in fact, would be the last time the group was ever mobbed by thousands of hysterical fans. Ringo and George arrived with their wives, but—as reporters were quick to note—the lady on John's arm was not Cynthia Lennon.

John first encountered the future love of his life in 1967, when he wandered into a friend's art gallery. On display was an exhibit by an experimental Japanese artist named Yoko Ono.

"I was astounded," Lennon remembers. "There was an apple on sale there for 200 quid [$500]. I thought it was fantastic. I got the humor in her work immediately. 200 quid to watch the apple decompose!"

The gallery owner suggested the struggling artist go "say hello to the millionaire. And she came up and handed me a card which said 'Breathe' on it. I just went (pant)."

John was easily talked into promising financial support for future Yoko Ono art shows. "Then I went to India with the Maharoonie and we were corresponding. The letters were still formal but they had a little side to them.

"When I got back from India we were talking to each other on the phone. I called her over, it was the middle of the night and Cyn was away, and I thought well now's the time if I'm ever going to get to know her any more. She came to the house and we went upstairs to my studio. I played her all the tapes that I'd made, all this far-out stuff. She was suitably impressed and then she said 'well let's make one ourselves' so we made *Two Virgins*." By the time they finished it a few hours later, says John, they realized they were in love.

The Lennon-Ono romance would soon become one of the most famous of the sixties. John had found in Yoko—who was seven years older than he—a partner, not only in love, but in his creative work as well. With her outrageous artistic flair, the Japanese banker's daughter seemed much more on John's wavelength than the modest, conventional Cynthia—or even, for that matter, Paul McCartney. Increasingly the Beatles would have to take a backseat in John's life to his activities with Yoko. If Brian Epstein's departure was the first nail in the group's coffin, then Yoko Ono's arrival was the second. According to John, he hoped at first "to carry on and just bring Yoko into our life. But it seemed that I had to either be married to them or Yoko, and I chose Yoko."

Yoko moved into John's $140,000 mansion in London's suburbs, and Cynthia was granted a divorce. When John put the house up for sale soon afterward, a London *Evening News* reporter came by, pretending he wanted to buy it. Instead, he shared this glimpse of John and Yoko's lifestyle with his readers: "Down the hallway, past piles of boxes, packages, floppy black hats, and books such as *The Geography of Witchcraft* and *The Vampire*, was the strangest room I ever entered. And why? It was made up of halves. Half a chair, half a table, half a radio, and even half an ironing board. Half a bookcase carried half-pots, half-pans, and half-kettles. The half-witted 'decorator' had even cut a single shoe in half. Nearly everything in the room had been painted white. The chessmen on a chess board were white. Both sets."

But reporters in search of a John and Yoko story hardly needed to sneak into their house to find one. The pair was highly visible, constantly staging "happenings," each one more offbeat than the last. Said Lennon: "I keep reading about Paul the brilliant melody writer and George the philosopher, so where does that leave me? Yes, that's right, the nut!"

He and Yoko made numerous films, including one of John's smile that lasted for ninety minutes. With great fanfare, the couple unveiled a "living art" sculpture outside Coventry Cathedral.

This consisted of two acorns planted for peace. The next morning it was discovered that overenthusiastic fans had spirited away the acorns during the night, but two more were soon found to replace them.

John took over a London gallery to present an exhibit of his own White Art. One highlight was an eight-foot circular canvas, all white except for the words "you are here" in tiny letters. Another was a helium machine that blew up white balloons all day long. Attached to each balloon was a tag, one side reading "you are here" and the other giving an address where the finder might "write to John Lennon." Clad all in white, the artist released his hundreds of balloons into the London skies with the words: "I declare these balloons high."

A lot of people did write back, but John was shocked at their negative message. Even many of the Beatles' fans seemed to view Yoko as a wicked witch, whose spell had sent the "brainy Beatle" clear off his rocker.

Paul and George did not, at first, take kindly to her, either. George informed John that Yoko gave off "bad vibes," and the fact that John was clearly more interested in Yoko's work than in Paul's made McCartney more than a bit jealous.

In the old days, the Beatles' wives and girl friends had been content to stay at home and prepare dinner while the boys worked on their masterpieces. But John's liberated woman insisted on being by his side at all times. When she felt unwell, she ordered a bed installed for her in the Beatles' recording studio. Yoko even—as John was the first to admit—"expected to perform with them like you would with any other group."

But since the Beatles weren't about to welcome Yoko as a fifth member, she and John decided to put out albums of their own. The first of these, *Two Virgins*, caused quite a flap—thanks entirely to the cover photograph showing the pair stark naked.

This particular Apple barely made it to the marketplace, as EMI and Capitol refused to touch it. A small "hip" company was finally talked into distributing *Two Virgins* in a brown-paper wrapper. Nonetheless, many dealers were arrested on charges of peddling smut. A New Jersey vice squad seized thirty thousand copies of the naughty LP.

The actual *Two Virgins* record was a collection of bird squawks, Yoko-squawks, backward tapes, and some tuneless piano playing. Few even of John's fans managed to sit through the whole thing.

On October 18, harsh reality intruded on John and Yoko's "love cloud"—in the form of the real-life Blue Meanies known as the Scotland Yard Drugs Squad. These uninvited guests dropped in with enormous police dogs, who promptly sniffed out what they were looking for. The couple was dragged to the nearest police station, where John pleaded guilty to possession of pot. Later, however, he claimed that the drugs had been planted, and that he had agreed to pay the $500 fine only to spare Yoko, newly pregnant, a long and painful court case. But a month later, she suffered a miscarriage anyway.

Apart from *Two Virgins*—which some of John's friends thought was the real reason for his arrest—Apple Records' first LP releases included several of interest to Beatle fans. There were two movie sound tracks: the Beatles' *Yellow Submarine*, and the rock 'n' raga instrumental music George had written for the film *Wonderwall*. Above all, there was a double album called, simply, *The Beatles*.

The new two LP set had been some six months in the making. It contained thirty new numbers, mostly written at the Maharishi's Indian retreat. Though some of these ranked among John, Paul, and George's finest, *The Beatles* hinted that the days of experimentation were pretty well over. For fans who had wondered whether the Beatles could ever top *Sgt. Pepper*, the answer was evidently that they weren't even going to try.

As songwriters, John and Paul were still growing—both up and apart. Lennon's work was more personal than ever, and McCartney's more polished. But as recording artists, John, Paul, George, and Ringo were starting to rest on their laurels. It was as if being members of the Beatles had finally become just an ordinary job for them. They handled the job like professional musicians, only the inspiration was beginning to run dry.

Gone now were most of the mysterious instruments, such as George's sitar, that had been featured in the last few albums. There were also fewer contributions from outside musicians. Psychedelia, in short, was out; and the emphasis was back on the Beatles' own voices, guitars, and drums. John suggested that the group was "coming out of a shell, kind of saying: remember what it was like to play." According to Paul: "We felt it was time to step back because that is what we wanted to do. You can still make good music without going forward. Some people want us to go on until we vanish up our own B-sides."

Actually, *The Beatles* boasted as much variety as ever—it practically amounted to an encyclopedia of every style of popular music—and only seemed simple in comparison with the Beatles' own few previous albums. But the cover could hardly have been more straightforward. In keeping with John's own White Art, it was completely blank—except for the embossed words "The BEATLES" and a number. (All copies of the White Album—as it came to be known—bore different numbers indicating the order in which they were printed: A1000000, for instance, was the millionth copy pressed in America.)

The White Album was certainly not a step back to the group's pre-*Rubber Soul* sound. For one thing, the writing, playing, and recording were much more sophisticated than on the early records. For another, *The Beatles*—despite the title—was hardly a group effort. John, Paul, and George each came to the studios with his own songs all worked out beforehand, and told the other members exactly what to play. For some numbers—such as Paul's "Why Don't We Do It in the Road?"—one lone Beatle would actually overdub himself playing all the instruments. Even when all the Beatles were working together, according to John, "it was just me and a backing group, Paul and a backing group. . . ." In a nutshell, *The Beatles* featured great Lennon songs, McCartney songs, and Harrison songs—plus Ringo Starr's "Don't Pass Me By"—but no Beatle songs.

They didn't even necessarily like each other's music anymore.

John, for instance, hated Paul's popular Jamaican-style sing-along "Obladi-Oblada." George, meanwhile, felt he was getting the short end of the stick. He was now writing as much material as John or Paul; and "Harrisongs" such as "While My Guitar Gently Weeps"—featuring guest guitarist Eric Clapton—were well up to the standards of Lennon and McCartney. But the Beatles' two original songwriters were used to hogging most of the space on the band's albums, and unwilling to make room for their junior partner. "My problem," says George, "is that it would always be very difficult to get in on the act, because Paul was very pushy in that respect. When he succumbed to playing on one of your tunes, he'd always do good. But you'd have to do 59 of Paul's songs before he'd even listen to one of yours." All signs pointed toward that day in the not so distant future when each Beatle would be free to make solo records—at the expense of the group's continuing existence.

Though there were no real Beatle songs on *The Beatles*, there were plenty of satires or parodies of just about every other group and style imaginable. Paul's "Back in the U.S.S.R.," for example, spoofed Chuck Berry—especially his "Back in the U.S.A."—and the Beach Boys. Elsewhere on the White Album, McCartney satirized everything from cowboy music and movies ("Rocky Raccoon") to scratchy old 78-rpm records ("Honey Pie"). John, meanwhile, took aim at the current British blues craze ("Yer Blues")—and even at the fanatical Beatle watchers who spent their time combing the group's records for hidden meanings and "clues." "Here's another clue for you all," Lennon wickedly sang in "Glass Onion"—and then went on to inform Beatle-obsessed sleuths that "the Walrus was Paul," that the Fool on the Hill is "living there still," and so forth. But few of the type of Beatle-maniac that John was making fun of seemed to get the joke.

One of those fanatics was Charles Manson, leader of a hippie commune in Southern California. Manson claimed to be Jesus Christ reborn, and imagined that the Beatles were the four long-haired angels prophesied in a part of the Bible called "Revelation 9." Each of the Beatles' records, he believed, was a personal message from the angels to the new Messiah, Charlie Manson.

When the White Album appeared with a piece titled "Revolution 9"—a collection of sound effects, including screams and gunfire, which John called his "drawing of revolution"—Manson grew even more convinced of his own farfetched and twisted theories. In Manson's view, the entire White Album was about a coming war between the races. Paul's "Blackbird," for instance, supposedly described black revolutionaries—whose white victims, according to Manson, were the subject of the next song on the album, George's "Piggies." Manson also found in the White Album a series of instructions on the role he and his followers were supposed to take in bringing this "revolution" about.

The Beatles' songs, therefore, were Manson's justification for killing such rich white "piggies" as Sharon Tate. At the scene of each of these gruesome murders, Manson's followers used the blood of their victims to write phrases from the White Album on the wall. Manson believed that white people would somehow think these horrors the work of black revolutionaries. The race war—"Helter Skelter"—would then follow, leaving Charlie and his followers to take control of what was left of the world.

Prosecutor Vincent Bugliosi titled *Helter Skelter*, his best-selling book on the Manson case, after the Beatles' song. In it, Bugliosi describes not only how the White Album helped him to solve the murder mystery—but also how difficult it was to convince the jury that it was not he who had taken leave of his senses. In any case, though Manson may have been the most dangerous lunatic ever to come down with Beatlemania, he was only one of many thousands who took the Beatles' every word incredibly seriously in the late sixties.

For those able to read between the lines a bit more logically than Charles Manson had, the real secret message of the White Album was that the Beatles were now individual artists with little left in common. "I enjoyed it," Lennon remembers, "but we broke up then."

7

Apple Corpse
(1969)

On the morning after New Year's Day 1969, the Beatles set up camp at Twickenham Film Studios outside London. As they started from scratch on a new album, to be called *Get Back*, cameramen were on hand to capture every Beatle gesture and note for a TV film on the making of this LP.

The words "Get Back"—also the title of one of the songs—summed up the intended spirit of the project. There were to be no outside musicians (except Billy Preston on piano and organ), no overdubbing or fancy electronic effects. *Get Back* would even include the sounds of the Beatles tuning up and chatting between numbers—plus bits of the rock-'n'-roll oldies with which they always warmed up before launching into their own material. Paul McCartney—whose brainwave all this was—wanted the album itself to have some of the documentary quality of the TV film that was being made about it.

To stress the LP's "back to the roots" theme, John and Paul decided to include "One After 909," a song they had written in 1958. For the cover photo, the Beatles—mostly sporting beards and shoulder-length hair—posed on the same housing-project balcony where, as clean-cut lads in matching suits, they had been photographed for their very first album jacket. (The two pictures were finally used back to back on the *1962–1966* and *1967–1970* "greatest hits" collections.) *Get Back*, promised *Beatles Monthly*, would "prove to those who thought the Beatles' studio ingenuity was getting TOO clever that they are still more than capable of turning out material EVERYONE can UNDERSTAND as well as enjoy."

The Beatles even announced plans to perform the new material at a special concert once the album was finished. Excited fans swamped *Beatles Monthly* with entries for a contest to win tickets. Paul dreamed of staging the show at an ancient coliseum in North Africa, or on a ship in the ocean. He felt that such a performance would make a terrific climax to the TV film.

John, George, and Ringo, however, found themselves unable to share Paul's enthusiasm. "We couldn't get into it," Lennon remembered two years later. "It was a dreadful, dreadful feeling in Twickenham Studio, being filmed all the time. You couldn't make music at eight in the morning, or ten or whatever it was, in a strange place with people filming you and colored lights."

McCartney tried to whip the band into shape with a pep talk: "We've been very negative since Mr. Epstein passed away. The only way for it not to be a bit of a drag is for the four of us to think: should we make it positive, or should we forget it. Mr. Epstein said sort of, 'get suits on,' and we did. We were always fighting that discipline a bit, but now it's silly to fight that discipline if it's our own. I think we need a bit more if we're going to get on with it."

"Well, if that's what 'doing it' is," snapped Harrison, "I don't want to do anything. I don't want to do the songs on a show because they always turn out awful like that. In the studio you can work on it until you get it how you want it."

George went on to describe the suggested sites for the concert as "very expensive and insane." There would be no way to get a decent sound on board ship, he complained, and as for the North African coliseum: "It would be impractical to try and get all these people and equipment there." The argument heated up to the point that John said he was beginning to think the show should be held at a lunatic asylum.

To demonstrate how much he was against the whole idea,

George stalked out of the studio and drove home. Plans for a Beatles show were scrapped, and the contest winners were sent LPs instead of concert tickets. For the climax of their film, the group simply took their equipment up on the roof of Apple. On January 30, in just about the only magical moment of the whole *Get Back* episode, the Beatles performed their new material to the crowd that quickly gathered on nearby rooftops. In the streets below, all traffic ground to a half. But these lucky Londoners' taste of live Beatle music was short-lived. Summoned by the head of a bank across the street, police put an end to the "disturbance."

"Get Back" was released as a single in April, and almost everyone agreed it was one of Paul's hottest rock 'n' roll numbers ever. But the rest of the album was a mess; and the Beatles left it to rot on the shelf along with the *Get Back* film. "None of us could be bothered going in," John later admitted. "There was 29 hours of tape because we were rehearsing and taping everything. Nobody could face looking at it. I really couldn't stand it."

The state of Apple Corps was also rotten. John discovered that the old friends the Beatles had put in charge of their company were "robbing us . . . just living and eating and drinking like Rome." Over $40,000 a week, he claimed, "was rolling out of Apple and nobody was doing anything about it. I suddenly realized we were losing money at such a rate that we would have been broke, really broke. It was just hell, and it had to stop."

All the Beatles agreed on the need for a tough manager to sort out the mess. "We're going to have to cut down a bit," said Ringo, "and do it properly as a business." To avoid winding up in the poorhouse, they were prepared to sacrifice much of what Apple was supposed to have stood for in the first place.

When John's cry for help made the newspapers, one of the first to respond was a New York wheeler-dealer named Allen Klein. Despite a snub from Brian Epstein, Klein had always dreamed of managing the Beatles—"because they're the best." For several years the blunt orphan who boasted "I don't have time to be polite" had had to settle for the Rolling Stones. But he closely followed the Beatles' career from his Times Square office.

Klein later told a *Playboy* magazine interviewer of "the moment I knew for sure that I was going to be their manager. I was driving across a bridge out of New York and I heard on the radio that Epstein had died and I said to myself, 'I got 'em.' " But he bided his time, waiting until the Beatles were over their heads in money troubles before making his move.

Three quarters of the Fab Four were impressed by this sharp operator who, according to John, "knew everything about us"— and who promised to get the Beatles the millions they felt they deserved. Paul McCartney, however, had very different ideas about who should be put in charge of the group's affairs.

In recent months, Paul's personal life had undergone a major change. He had parted ways with Jane Asher; and, when in New York to promote Apple, had met a blonde photographer named Linda Eastman. At the time, the lovely Linda was considered something of a groupie, known to go out with numerous rock stars. But friends who thought her romance with Paul would be as short-lived as her other flings were proven wrong. Linda and her young daughter, Heather, were soon invited to move in with rock's most glamorous bachelor—and they never left.

Though a familiar face on the New York rock 'n' roll scene, Linda came from a highly respectable and wealthy background. Her father, Lee, was a top music business lawyer (and art collector), and brother John had followed in their father's footsteps to become his partner. Naturally it occurred to Paul that Eastman & Eastman should get a crack at solving the Beatles' financial troubles.

Both Klein and the Eastmans were invited to take part in the complicated negotiations that drained much of the Beatles' energy throughout 1969. Despite their combined efforts, the boys lost control of the company that published their music, and were also forced to pay a small fortune to break their ties with a management company originally set up by Epstein. But, thanks to Klein's wheeling and dealing, a new contract with EMI and Capitol made the Beatles the highest-paid act in record-business history.

Allen Klein and Lee Eastman, however, soon proved incapable of working together. Ugly words were exchanged in front of the four Beatles, who found themselves increasingly drawn into the battle. John developed a strong dislike for Eastman, whom he viewed as an insincere "middle-class pig." Paul had an equally low opinion of the coarse-mannered Klein. But, because the other two tended to side with Lennon, Klein was installed, over McCartney's protests, as business manager of Apple.

The atmosphere at the Beatles' company quickly changed from that of a freaks' paradise to the everyday air of an ordinary business. Klein's appearance struck terror in the hearts of Apple's employees, many of whom were sent packing. The likes of Magic Alex, with his fruit-shaped radios and nothing boxes, were among the first to go. Those allowed to stay on were forced to make do without the fat expense accounts and other fringe benefits.

Klein even shut down a short-lived second Beatles' record company called Zapple Records. This had been introduced as a "paperback records concept." All Zapple releases were to be cheaply priced albums which people were supposed to listen to once or twice and then throw away. But the only ones that made it to the stands were John and Yoko's *Unfinished Music No. 2* and George Harrison's *Electronic Sound*. (This last featured George's first attempts to play with his new toy, a moog synthesizer.) Klein dealt Zapple a death blow with the words: "If it's good we'll charge."

After Klein's rise to power, McCartney was seldom seen at the offices of the company that used to be his own brainchild. One of his few appearances anywhere in the public eye was on March 12—when he and Linda "made it official." A crowd of weeping girls gathered in the rain to watch the last of the bachelor Beatles leave the civic ceremony with his new wife.

That very night George Harrison's psychedelic bungalow was raided by the same Sergeant Pilcher who had masterminded the

Lennon drug bust six months earlier. Once again a few grains of pot were found in the home of a Beatle, and once again there were accusations that it had all been a setup. Because of his involvement with Indian religion and meditation, said George, "any sort of drugs is out. I haven't taken anything like that personally for a long time. Even before I got busted I never took it [pot], it just happened that they seemed to bring it with them that day."

George was developing a close relationship with the Hare Krishna movement—though he did draw the line at shaving his head and giving up "ciggies." Harrison even presented the London branch of the Radha Krishna Temple with an Apple recording contract. Their first Harrison-produced single, naturally, was "Hare Krishna." When Lennon ran into Apple's newest group, he asked them whether their record would make Number One. "Higher than that," they replied. ("Hare Krishna" actually made it to number 12 on the British charts.)

Eight days after the McCartney wedding, John and Yoko, in Paris on vacation, chartered a plane to the British colony of Gibraltar, Spain. With no advance warning the couple—dressed in white right down to their sneakers—got married themselves. Then the newlyweds flew straight back to Paris. John told reporters that he and Yoko originally "didn't believe in getting married"—until it occurred to them that they could turn their honeymoon into a "fantastic happening." Added Yoko: "You'll know soon enough what it is."

A few days later, the Lennons checked in at the Amsterdam Hilton. Fifty reporters were invited up to their room, to find John and Yoko sprawled in bed, each holding a Dutch tulip. The happening, the pair announced, was that they were going to lie in bed for a week, growing their hair for peace. "This," said John, "is our protest against all the suffering and violence in the world."

Some newspaper writers charged that the Lennons were making a mockery of serious protests against war and injustice. John insisted he was sincere and said he hoped to be remembered, not so much for his music, but "as a great peacenik." Yet he added, "Our policy is not to be taken too seriously. All the serious people like Martin Luther King and Kennedy got shot. We're willing to be the world's clowns."

Other newspapers said John and Yoko were fast becoming the world's bores—while continuing to run such headlines as "Day Two of the Lennon Lie-In ... John and Yoko forced out by Maria, the Hotel Maid." Letters to the editor poured in: "How could you permit that disgusting photograph? It is bad enough when valuable space is given to reporting the antics of these creatures." "I see John Lennon considers his lie-in 'the best idea we've had yet.' So what? I have the same idea every morning—when the alarm clock rings!"

Following their week in bed, the Lennons made a lightning trip to Vienna to see one of their films shown on Austrian TV. They offered another happening at a press conference, throughout which the couple remained hidden in a large bag on top of a table. John described this as a new form of communication called "bagism." "People were saying 'C'mon, get out of the bag.' And we wouldn't let 'em see us. It was just great."

The next morning—April Fool's Day—John and Yoko caught the early plane back to London, holding fifty acorns tied in a sack. They planned to send an acorn to each of the world's top leaders, with the request that it be planted for peace.

John immediately set the story of his unusual honeymoon to music. He was so pleased with his "Ballad of John and Yoko" and its Fifties sound that he demanded it be recorded and released at once on a new Beatles single.

Lennon was not to be put off by the fact that "Get Back" had only just hit the stands, or that he couldn't get hold of either Ringo—who was filming The Magic Christian with Peter Sellers—or George. Paul was persuaded to overdub himself playing drums, and John did the honors on piano and lead guitar.

Even so, "Ballad of John and Yoko" hit a snag when many American Top Forty stations refused to play a song with the chorus Christ you know it ain't easy. (Others merely bleeped out the word "Christ.") The lack of airplay kept the single from rising any higher than number eight. John insisted he was actually "Christ's biggest fan." But he added: "Yes, I still think it. Kids are more influenced by us than by Jesus."

The Lennons' honeymoon was also celebrated on yet a third LP of their "unfinished music." One whole side of their *Wedding Album* consisted of John and Yoko repeating each other's names for twenty-two minutes; the other featured tapes of the Amsterdam lie-in. The record was packaged with a piece of plastic wedding cake, and a book of press clippings about the Lennons' adventures. One of these articles sadly suggested that "a man who found fame and fortune in the evolution of a new sound, a bright image in a dull world, and a not inconsiderable musical talent . . . seems to have come perilously near to having gone off his rocker."

Despite the nay-sayers, John and Yoko intended to stage an American lie-in to protest the Vietnam war. But United States officials refused to let the Beatle into the country on the grounds that he had a criminal drug record. The pair were obliged to settle for ten days in a Montreal bed, where they were still able to attract a great deal of coverage from U.S. television, radio, and newspapers.

While in bed John wrote a new song called "Give Peace a Chance," and immediately ordered a mobile recording studio installed in his hotel room. All his visitors—who at that particular moment included Timothy Leary, Tommy Smothers, a rabbi, and Montreal's branch of the Radha Krishna Temple—were asked to clap their hands and sing along. John christened this rag-tag group "the Plastic Ono Band" and directed that "Give Peace a Chance" be released as an Apple single without delay. The song quickly became something of an anthem for the antiwar movement. John has said that the most moving experience of his life was hearing "Give Peace a Chance" on the evening news, chanted in Washington by tens of thousands of peace demonstrators.

While John and Yoko grabbed all the headlines by turning

their every move into a public "happening," Paul and Linda just about vanished from the world's view. But over the summer of 1969 McCartney came out of his shell to coax Lennon, Harrison, and Starr back into EMI's Abbey Road recording studios for what would turn out to be the very last time.

Like seasoned pros, the Beatles polished off a new album in a matter of weeks. Named after the London street where they had made nearly all their famous recordings, *Abbey Road* showed the group making a final, heroic effort to ignite the Beatles magic despite the growing musical and personality differences. The LP was their first in years to feature all four boys on just about every song. As Ringo put it: "It's more important that we play good together than to have lots of violins play good together." *Abbey Road* also boasted more three-part harmony singing than any other Beatles album. As singers and musicians, John, Paul, George, and Ringo had never sounded so good.

The songs themselves featured the oddest cast of Beatle characters yet: "Mean Mr. Mustard" and his sister "Polythene Pam," plus the rascally Maxwell who delights in bumping people off with his magic hammer. That song, explained Paul, was about "the downfalls in life. Just when everything is going smoothly 'bang bang' down comes Maxwell's silver hammer and ruins everything." But John detested this sort of cabaret-style McCartney number, which he sarcastically called "nice little folk songs for the grannies to dig." Years later George also complained: "Paul would make us do these really fruity songs. I mean, my God, 'Maxwell's Silver Hammer' was so fruity!"

Most of Paul's work on *Abbey Road*, however, was saved for the ambitious song medley that takes up the last fifteen minutes of side two. That, said George Martin, "was Paul and I getting together. I was trying to make a symphony out of pop music, trying to get Paul to write stuff that referred back to something else. Bring some form to the thing."

According to Martin, "Paul really dug what I was trying to do," and wanted to weave the whole album into a "pop symphony." John, however, "hated that—he liked good old rock 'n'

Paul McCartney with his new
wife, Linda, and stepdaughter,
Heather, after the wedding
(*Popperfoto*)

George Harrison with his friends from the Radha Krishna Temple
—Apple's newest recording stars (*Keystone Press Agency*)

The Lennons' Dutch honeymoon took the
form of an antiwar "lie-in" (*Popperfoto*)

Three bearded Beatles could be spotted in the audience
at Bob Dylan's concert on the Isle of Wight (*Popperfoto*)

roll. So *Abbey Road* was a compromise. Side One was a collection of individual songs."

"I liked the 'A' side," agreed John, "but I never liked that sort-of pop opera on the other side. I think it's junk because it was just bits of songs thrown together. 'Come Together' is all right, that's all I remember. That was *my* song."

The publishers of Chuck Berry's music, however, thought it sounded like one of *their* songs, and sued John for having lifted "Come Together"'s tune from Berry's "You Can't Catch Me." (The dispute was eventually settled when Lennon agreed to record the Berry tune on one of his solo albums.)

"Come Together"'s words, at least, were highly original—and there was little mistaking the identity of the long-haired Walrus from Bag Productions whom they described. "Come Together" proved that John had not totally lost his love of words or sense of fun—two qualities often missing from the increasingly direct and personal material Lennon was now writing. "Whatever I'm singing I really mean," said John. "I don't mess about."

To many listeners, it was George Harrison who was the real hero of *Abbey Road*. Along with some really fine guitar playing, George contributed the album's two most popular songs. "Here Comes the Sun," he said, "was from the same period as Paul's song 'You Never Give Me Your Money.' We'd had meetings and meetings on bankers and lawyers and contracts and shares, and it was really awful because it's not the sort of thing we enjoy. One day I didn't come into the office, it was like slagging off school, and I went to Eric Clapton's house in the country. It was a really nice day and I picked up the guitar for the first time in a couple of weeks. The first thing that came out was that song."

The sun was certainly shining on George's career. His other *Abbey Road* number, "Something," was released by popular demand as a single. "They blessed me with a couple of B-sides in the past," said George, "but this is the first time I've had an A-side. Big deal, eh?"

As a single, this beautiful "Harrisong" became one of the

Beatles' all-time American best-sellers, and it has also been re-corded by more different artists than any Lennon-McCartney song except "Yesterday." One of these was Frank Sinatra, who called George's ballad "the greatest love song of the past 50 years." The "quiet Beatle" could hardly be blamed for thinking he had earned the right to more than two songs per album.

Shortly after *Abbey Road's* early October release, America was swept by the most bizarre of all Beatle rumors: Paul McCartney, it was whispered, was dead.

The weird tale was first aired over a Detroit FM station. An agitated listener phoned disk jockey Russ Gibb to tell him about the strange pattern formed by many of the mysterious mum-blings and sound effects on the Beatles' records, some of which had to be played backward for the "clues" to emerge. Gibb fol-lowed the caller's instructions, and found that John Lennon did indeed seem to say "I bury Paul" at the end of "Strawberry Fields." When he played parts of the White Album backward, the words "number nine, number nine" (on "Revolution 9") be-came, apparently, "turn me on dead man, turn me on dead man"; and the muttering at the end of "I'm So Tired" sounded suspi-ciously like "Paul is dead, man, miss him, miss him."

A few days later, *The Michigan Daily* printed a gruesome re-view of *Abbey Road.* Illustrated with a picture of McCartney's se-vered head, it read more like an obituary. The LP cover, it claimed, shows the Beatles leaving a cemetery, dressed as a min-ister (John), an undertaker (Ringo), and a grave digger (George). Paul, out of step with the others, holds a cigarette in his right hand—proof positive that this is actually a double for the left-handed McCartney. He is also barefoot, which, according to the article, is how corpses are often buried in England. The creepy symbolism supposedly extended even to the parked Volkswagen seen in the photograph. Its license plate number, 28 IF, meant Paul would have been 28 IF still alive. (McCartney was actually twenty-seven, but nobody thought of that.)

The article also dragged in "evidence" from earlier LP covers. *Sgt. Pepper* shows a grave, with flowers planted in the shape of

132

Paul's bass guitar. A hand is extended over McCartney's head in an omen of death. The booklet of pictures in *Magical Mystery Tour* includes one of Paul sitting in front of a sign that reads "I WAS." In another photograph, three of the Beatles are shown wearing red carnations; Paul's, however, is black.

As the rumor snowballed across the country, literally hundreds of new clues were found, both on the LP covers and in the songs themselves. Amateur detectives by the thousands joined in the new craze of playing Beatles records backward and at different speeds.

The "Paul Is Dead" fans generally agreed that the tragedy occurred on the night of November 9, 1966—a "stupid bloody Tuesday." McCartney, driving his Aston Martin—a model of which sits in a doll's lap on the *Sgt. Pepper* cover—"blew his mind out in a car." (Sound effects of a car crash can be heard on "Revolution 9.") Paul's head was severed from his body, and the Beatle was Officially Pronounced Dead on "Wednesday morning at five o'clock." (On the back of the *Pepper* cover, in a photo in which Paul's back is turned, George's hand points out this phrase from "She's Leaving Home." On the inside sleeve, McCartney wears an armpatch that says O.P.D.—for Officially Pronounced Dead.)

John, George, and Ringo, the story went, decided to carry on with a McCartney look-alike contest winner filling the dead Beatle's shoes. To let the world in on their secret, they chose the subtle method of planting clues on all their records.

At the time, many people actually believed all this. Apple's switchboard was jammed with long-distance calls from weeping American fans. But neither Apple nor Capitol made much of an effort to squash the rumors entirely; the record companies were perfectly aware of the millions of fresh copies of the "evidence" being snapped up at record shops by all those amateur sleuths. Thanks in part to McCartney's "death," *Abbey Road* became the biggest-selling Beatles album ever.

Eventually Paul himself emerged from his Scotland hideaway to tell reporters: "Rumors of my death are greatly exaggerated. If

I were dead I'd be the last to know." But even many of those willing to believe this *was* McCartney and not his double were still convinced that the Beatles had "buried Paul" between the lines of their songs on purpose as an elaborate practical joke.

John, however, insisted that the list of "death clues" was as much a figment of Beatlemaniacs' imaginations as Charlie Manson's "Helter Skelter" theories had been. "The whole thing was made up. We wouldn't do anything like that. People have nothing better to do than study Bibles and study rocks and make stories about how people used to live and all that. You know, it's just something to do for them, they live vicariously."

McCartney's out-of-character absence from the London scene and from the public eye had no doubt contributed to talk of his "death." Hurt by the loss of John to Yoko, and of Apple Corps to Allen Klein, Paul concentrated on building a new life with Linda and their new baby, Mary. No longer the swinging "bachelor Beatle," McCartney had become the most conservative and family-oriented of the four.

Lennon, meanwhile, soldiered on with his extraordinary peace campaign. Its most exciting moment was his first concert appearance in over three years. This came about when the producer of a giant outdoors concert in Toronto telephoned John two days before the September 13 show to offer free front-row seats and round-trip plane tickets. He accepted—on condition that the Plastic Ono Band be allowed to perform on stage "Give Peace a Chance." But after rounding up guitarist Eric Clapton, drummer Andy White, and bassist Klaus Voorman (the Beatles' friend from the Hamburg days), Lennon almost chickened out of his spur-of-the-moment commitment. The new improved Plastic Ono Band barely made the last possible flight to Toronto.

Seldom has a rock show been so electric with tension and suspense. The tens of thousands of fans had no idea what to expect from a real live Beatle—and neither did John or his Plastic Ono Band, who hadn't even had time to rehearse. Lennon was so nervous that he threw up before walking on stage. But he needn't have worried about the crowd, which went wild at the mere sound of John's Liverpool accent when he announced: "We're just gonna do numbers that we know, 'cause we've never played together before."

Lennon's all-star band turned out raw but powerful performances of "Money," "Dizzy Miss Lizzy," "Yer Blues," and—"this is what we came for really"—"Give Peace a Chance." Then Yoko crawled out of a large white bag to offer half an hour of the blood-curdling screams that had become her specialty. Though many agreed with the *Rolling Stone* critic who said Yoko's music sounded "like a severely retarded child being tortured," her devoted husband was convinced it was as good as "Paul and Dylan rolled into one." The entire performance was captured on an Apple LP called *Live Peace in Toronto 1969.*

John's short set also included a remarkable new number called "Cold Turkey." "I wrote this," said Lennon, "about coming off drugs and the pain involved." The music was as harsh and unpleasant as the message, for John was no longer interested in creating nice images and pretty tunes to entertain and soothe his listeners. His new songs laid bare the inner torment of an artist who considered it his task to be as honest and as true to life as possible.

"Hey, lads, I think I've written a new single," said John to the other Beatles. But McCartney was less than delighted with the idea—or the song—so Lennon went ahead and recorded "Cold Turkey" with Ringo Starr, Klaus Voorman, and Eric Clapton as a Plastic Ono Band release. John got back at his long-time partner by refusing to credit the tune to "Lennon-McCartney"—thereby putting an end to the joint billing that had always been used even for songs they had written separately.

The second Plastic Ono Band single, however, was something of a flop on the charts. This annoyed John so much that when he returned his M.B.E. to the queen a few weeks later as a protest against Britain's involvement in the Nigerian war and its support of the United States in Vietnam, he included "Cold Turkey" 's poor sales among his reasons for sending back the medal. The disrespect John showed in throwing away one of his country's greatest honors upset more patriotic Britons than the Beatles' having been given it in the first place. Many who did share John's political views could not make sense of his having put the fate of one of his own records on the same level as that of war-torn Nigeria and Vietnam.

Even his Aunt Mimi—upon whose TV set John's medal had rested for the past four years—told a reporter: "I cannot agree that this is any way to register a protest. If I'd known what he wanted to do with it, I would not have let him have his M.B.E."

"I'm very upset that my Auntie Mimi is upset," declared Lennon. "I will ring her to try and explain why I handed the M.B.E. back. She doesn't understand half the things that I do. She hasn't yet got over the fact that I started wearing sideburns when I was 18."

John's next move was to spread his new slogan "WAR IS OVER! IF YOU WANT IT" through full-page newspaper ads and billboards in most of the world's major cities. He even tried to replace the Christian calendar by announcing: "Everyone who's into peace will regard the New Year [A.D. 1970] as Year One A.P., for After Peace. All our letters and calendars from now on will use this method."

Lennon began pouring his energies into organizing a huge Woodstock-style Peace Festival in Toronto. But the producers he chose to work with proved overly out of touch with reality, even for Lennon's taste. When they passed the word that not only the Beatles and Bob Dylan, but also a fleet of UFO's, were all slated to appear at the Peace Fest, John decided to forget the whole idea.

Instead, he launched 1970 (or Year One, as he called it) by auctioning off all his hair for the Black Power movement, and by recording a third Plastic Ono Band single with the legendary early Sixties producer Phil Spector. "Instant Karma" (unlike "Cold Turkey") was a huge hit.

George, meanwhile, made a low-profile return to the concert stage as guest guitarist for an American band, Delaney and Bonnie. On those rare occasions when the four Beatles crossed paths, their meetings produced further arguments but no new music. At one point John stunned Paul with the words: "I want a divorce."

McCartney and Klein joined forces for once, to persuade Lennon not to say anything publicly. "There was a lot to do businesswise," John later admitted. "It would not have been suitable at the time. Paul and Allen said they were glad I wasn't going to announce it. Paul said: 'Oh well, that means nothing really happened if you're not going to say anything.' "

All the Beatles did agree to John's suggestion that Phil Spector be allowed to turn the *Get Back* LP tapes into a marketable record. "He worked like a pig on it," Lennon remembers. "He'd always wanted to work with the Beatles." The *Get Back* film, meanwhile, was edited for release as a feature-length movie instead of a TV special; and both record and film were retitled *Let It Be.*

With or without Phil Spector, *Let It Be* remains the least satisfying of all Beatles albums. This is partly because the songs are by no means their best; and the Beatles themselves were in such poor spirits when they recorded them. But *Let It Be* also suffers from Spector's inability to decide whether to turn it into a polished production, or keep the casual and intimate atmosphere that the original plans for *Get Back* had called for. The between-song chatter remained on the album, but Spector also added orchestras and choirs to the Beatles' "back to the roots" music. The combination sounded ridiculous.

The movie showed a rare glimpse of the Beatles at work on an LP—and what wouldn't any Beatlemaniac have given to see a film on the making of *Revolver* or *Sgt. Pepper?* It was just a shame the movie had to be about the Beatles' most depressing record. The rooftop concert, however, made it well worth the price of admission.

While Spector patched together *Let It Be,* McCartney busied himself in the recording studio he had built on his Scottish farm. Overdubbing all the instruments himself, he produced the first real solo album by any of the Beatles. Having kept the whole operation top secret, Paul arrived in London to arrange for Apple's prompt release of his *McCartney* LP.

The other three Beatles tried to delay Paul's record, on the grounds that *McCartney* would damage the sales of *Let It Be* if both were released at the same time. Paul felt the others were ganging up on him. When Ringo turned up to press their argument, Paul threw him out of the house with the words: "I'll finish you all." "While I thought he had behaved like a spoiled child," said Ringo, "I could see that the release date of his record had a gigantic emotional significance to him, and felt we should let him have his way."

They did, but by this time Paul had finally given up hope of keeping the Beatles going. As part of the *McCartney* package, he prepared a self-interview containing the message that would stun the world. On April 10, 1970, newspaper headlines trumpeted McCartney's decision to "break with the Beatles." He gave his reasons as "personal differences, musical differences, business differences, but most of all because I have a better time with my family. . . . My plan," announced Paul, "is to grow up."

To the other Beatles, the only surprise about the breakup was that it had been McCartney who'd made it official. According to John, "He rang me up that day and said, 'I'm doing what you and Yoko are doing, I'm putting out an album and I'm leaving the group *too.*' I was feeling a little strange because *he* was saying it this time, and I said good because he was the one that wanted the Beatles most. And then the midnight papers came out. I was a fool not to do what Paul did, which was use it to sell a record. He's about the best P.R. man in the world, he really does a job."

"The cartoon is this," cracked John at the time. "Four guys on stage with a spotlight on them. Second picture, three guys breezing out of the spotlight. Third picture, one guy standing there shouting 'I'm leaving.'"

Most Beatlemaniacs liked to think all this was just a family squabble, soon to be smoothed over. But they were wrong.

8

Solo in the Seventies

Paul McCartney—Beatle on the Wing

When it sank in that the Beatles had indeed broken up—perhaps for good—people tended to blame one or another of several "villains." Some held Allen Klein or the Eastmans responsible. Others blamed Linda or Yoko—to which John angrily responded: "How can two women break up four strong men? It's impossible." But because it was Paul who had made the split official, it was Paul who wound up taking most of the heat from angry fans and critics.

Years later McCartney would enjoy more favorable publicity and record sales than any of the other Beatles. But this was far from the case in the very early seventies, when John and George seemed to share most of the hits and the glory.

Both Lennon and Harrison continued to see themselves as serious artists, with an important message to share with the world. But Paul apparently decided—once he put the Beatles behind him—that the purpose of his music was simply to entertain.

The *McCartney* album was mostly a mixture of old songs the Beatles had never used, and tunes Paul admittedly "ad-libbed on the spot" while playing around in his home studio with the tape recorder running. Only "Maybe I'm Amazed" seemed up to the standard of his Beatles songs, though the rest made for perfectly pleasant background music. Those who had hoped McCartney's musical "Declaration of Independence" would live up to the promise of his *Abbey Road* "Pop Symphony" were bound to feel disappointed.

Paul himself summed up *McCartney* as a simple celebration of "home, family, love." Not for the last time, his record jacket was covered with snapshots of the McCartneys romping with their children and pets along tropical beaches and on their own country estate. Many rock writers were nauseated by Paul's new image as a prosperous—and "straight"—family man. This, together with his unadventurous songs and his role in the Beatles breakup, caused him to be called a sellout—a traitor to everything his old band and the sixties rock culture were supposed to have stood for.

At the end of 1970, McCartney took the other Beatles to court to have their partnership legally dissolved. He did this mainly to free himself from the clutches of Allen Klein, but the public saw it as further proof that Paul was responsible for destroying the Beatles. John, George, and Ringo defended themselves in court with statements portraying Paul as the villain of the piece; Ringo, for example, told how Paul had threatened him and thrown him out of the house. McCartney eventually won the lawsuit anyway; but all that publicly aired dirty laundry only increased the bitterness between him and the other ex-Beatles.

Paul tried to bounce back into the world's favor with a new album. *Ram* was much more polished than *McCartney*, but despite some snatches of fine music there were still no great songs in the Beatles sense. The rock critics, out for blood, tore *Ram* to pieces.

"I thought *McCartney* was quite good," said Paul. "But then it didn't quite do it in every way. It was very down-home, funky, just me. After it got knocked, I thought, do just the opposite next time. So *Ram* was with the top people in the top studio. I thought, *this* is what they want. But again, it was critically panned."

The dreadful reviews made even Paul wonder whether the McCartney magic had gone stale. Perhaps he had grown out of touch on his own, and needed to build another close working relationship with other musicians. He decided to form a new band.

Paul McCartney and Wings on their
European bus tour (*Popperfoto*)

At the very least, this would enable him to realize his dream of playing before live audiences again.

The rock world had a good laugh over the lineup of Paul's band, which he called Wings. Joining former Moody Blues guitarist Denny Laine and New York session drummer Denny Seiwell was none other than Linda McCartney—who had never played an instrument before—on piano and vocals. Of Linda's talents, one critic said: "She couldn't carry a tune in a bucket." But Paul—who had already billed *Ram* as a "Paul and Linda McCartney" album—apparently hoped to challenge the headline-grabbing Lennons with a husband-wife team of his own.

Hot on the heels of *Ram*, Wings rushed out an LP called *Wild Life*. This, unfortunately, turned out to be the poorest of all McCartney's post-Beatle albums. Paul needed more time to rehearse his band and write new material; and *Wild Life*, far from correcting the impression that McCartney had lost his talent, only made matters worse. The music was uninspired and sloppily performed, and the words those of a man who had little to say and said it badly. One rock magazine wished Wings a "crash landing" in its 1971 list of Christmas "gifts" to the stars.

Despite the music world's scorn, Paul stubbornly pursued his new career as a member of Wings. To fill out the band's sound, Henry McCullough was added on lead guitar. On February 9, 1972—the eighth anniversary of the Beatles' historic "Ed Sullivan Show" appearance—Wings turned up unannounced at Nottingham University, to play their first concert to a few hundred students.

Over the next few weeks, the band bombed around Britain in a van, playing intimate shows at university ballrooms and cafeterias. Most of these were arranged at a few hours' notice, to make sure no reporters would turn up. This was actually a scheme Paul had dreamed up for the Beatles in 1969, only to be shot down by John. It enabled Paul's group to polish their act before small, off-the-beaten-track audiences too thrilled at the presence of a live Beatle on campus to be overly critical if the performance didn't quite measure up to the myth.

During the summer of 1972, McCartney spread his Wings across Europe. Traveling in a colorfully repainted London double-decker bus, the band visited nine countries ranging from the sunny south of France to subarctic Finland. The magical mystery tour hit a snag in Sweden, where Paul was arrested and fined $2,000 for the possession of pot. The unpleasant incident, however, did wonders for the fuddy-duddy image Paul had taken on in the minds of some of his old admirers. A few months later he was actually busted again, for growing marijuana at his Scotland farm.

In the spring of 1973, Paul finally worked up enough confidence to do a "proper" tour of his own country. He now had a well-oiled, professional act—though the off-key singing of his highly visible wife did continue to draw an occasional boo. But the shows' most glaring flaw was the absence of any of Paul's best songs—those he had written for the Beatles. Singing them, he said later, "would have been too painful, like reliving some kind of weird dream." But Wings' own releases thus far were hardly in the same category—certainly not their pathetic single, "Mary Had a Little Lamb," which featured the old nursery rhyme set to a new tune.

The music, however, began to improve with Wings' second LP, *Red Rose Speedway*, released in time for the British tour. Though far from earthshaking, this was a charming and well-produced collection of the "silly love songs" to which Paul had chosen to devote his talents. *Speedway* and its resident single "My Love"—exactly the sort of McCartney ballad that unfriendly critics called "saccharine"—gave Wings their first U.S. Number Ones.

Always—as George Harrison put it—"the workaholic" of the Beatles, Paul was once again bursting with plans and ideas. "It became a challenge to me," he said. "Either I was going to go under or I was going to get something together." One of his projects was a rather cutesy-pie TV special called *James Paul McCartney*. Another was his assignment to write the theme music for the James Bond film *Live and Let Die*. The "hip" press deemed it a sellout for an ex-Beatle to get involved with a slick, show-bizzy thriller; *Rolling Stone* broke the news with a snide paragraph that concluded: "So it's come to that." Still, Paul performed his secret-agent mission most effectively, and "Live and Let Die" gave Wings another million-selling single.

Wings, at last, had arrived. Or—more accurately—Paul McCartney had returned. The ex-Beatle managed to convince nobody that Wings were in fact a four-man—plus-one-woman—*band* with an identity all its own—which, Paul insisted, had no connection with that other group he had once played with but now pretended not to remember. In any case, this fiction was rudely shattered just days before Wings' scheduled departure for recording sessions in—of all places—Lagos, Nigeria. Tired of being bossed around by Paul, Henry McCullough and Denny Seiwell suddenly quit the band. The McCartneys caught their African flight anyway, joined only by the ever faithful Denny Laine.

The disastrous circumstances forced Paul to overdub guitars and drums himself—along with his usual assortment of bass, piano, organ, and synthesizer. Some African drummers were also hired—which led to charges that the ex-Beatle was trying to rip off the natives' music. On top of it all, Paul was robbed at gunpoint by bandits.

Miraculously, all this served to shake McCartney clear of his musical rut. According to Linda, "Paul thought: I've *got* to do it, either I give up and cut my throat or I get my magic back." He did indeed rise to the occasion, by producing an LP absolutely chockful of uplifting melodies in the best McCartney tradition. Released at the end of 1973, *Band on the Run* was seen in some circles as a "concept album," with every song following the theme of escape, flight, and freedom.

Rolling Stone hailed McCartney's "creation of a fantasy world of adventure . . . uniting the myth of the rock star and the outlaw, the original legendary figure On the Run"—and welcomed Paul back to the fold with an Album-of-the-Year award. *Band on the Run* went on to outsell every other LP ever made by an ex-Beatle.

Though other Wings albums would lack the magic of Paul's African adventure, McCartney never again lost his knack for turning out hit records.

Paul eventually found two new Wings: pint-sized twenty-one-year-old guitarist Jimmy McCulloch; and Joe English, an American drummer. The next album, *Venus and Mars*, was recorded in New Orleans. The reviews were not as good as those for *Band on the Run*, but *Venus and Mars'* sales were only a shade less astronomical.

In 1975, McCartney worked up a fresh act, based around the new album. Along with such *Venus and Mars* hits as "Listen to What the Man Said," he saw fit to treat his British audiences to a few choice Beatles oldies, including "Lady Madonna," "Blackbird," and "Yesterday." "They're great tunes," said Paul. "So I just decided in the end, this isn't such a big deal, I'll do them." Now that the world had accepted his new music, Paul was able to come to terms with his past.

In 1976, after ironing out visa problems caused by his marijuana arrests, Paul was at last ready to take his act to the United States. The "Wings Over America" tour was an instant sellout, with tickets changing hands for $100 on the black market. Four years of touring Britain, Europe, and Australia had helped McCartney to polish his show into one of the most exciting and professional extravaganzas ever known to rock. American fans were not disappointed.

During the "Venus and Mars" opener, hundreds of bubbles floated down over Wings—who then disappeared slowly in a cloud of artifical mist. "Live and Let Die" was livened up by a lethal display of laser beams and blinding mushroom clouds. For the thirties-style "You Gave Me the Answer," pink and yellow light bulbs flashed from Paul's piano.

But the real treat was in the music. Paul's voice alternately crooned and belted, soaring to notes most rock singers don't even know exist. His all-around instrumental talent was in excellent form as he bounced from bass to piano to organ. But the show's clincher came when the other Wings left McCartney to sit alone with his acoustic guitar, to croon "Blackbird" and "Yester-day" to the hushed crowd. The triumphant tour was recorded and filmed for a live three-LP album and a TV special—both ti-tled *Wings Over America.*

In recent years, McCartney has continued to enjoy a string of Number One hits, such as "Silly Love Songs" and "With a Little Luck." In 1979, he even made a disco record, "Goodnight To-night," widely seen as further proof that the Beatle who had once helped in setting so many trends was now content merely to fol-low them. Paul continued the tradition of recording Wings albums in unusual locations: 1978's *London Town* was made on a yacht in the Caribbean Sea; and 1979's *Back to the Egg* in a castle overlooking the English Channel. But critics complained that there was nothing unusual about the music itself.

McCartney did, however, record one very special single. This was 1977's "Mull of Kintyre," a tribute to the misty landscape surrounding his beloved Scotland farm. Performed in the style of a Scottish folk song—complete with bagpipes—"Mull of Kin-tyre" became the biggest-selling record *ever* released in Britain. But, in the strangest McCartney mystery since the 1969 death hoax, the single was a total flop in the United States.

By this time, Joe English and Jimmy McCulloch—who would be found dead in 1979 at the age of twenty-six—had both flown the coop. Paul eventually replaced them with Steve Holly (drums) and Laurence Juber (guitar). Columbia Records lured the new Wings away from Capitol with a record-breaking deal said to put up to $24 million in the ex-Beatle's pocket.

Paul McCartney is now the richest musician in the world. In 1979, the *Guinness Book of World Records* awarded him a rhodium record—made out of the world's most precious metal—for being the most successful recording artist of all time. Paul has even turned into a music-business tycoon, investing his money in buying the rights to the songs of his old hero Buddy Holly—plus such hit Broadway scores as *Annie.* Yet, unlike the other ex-Bea-tles, McCartney is still at his old job full time, working harder than ever. "I kind of just drive in," he says, "make music all day, drive back, go to sleep, get up, drive in, make music all day."

When Paul does take a well-earned day off, he prefers to spend it at home, with Linda and the four kids—Heather, Mary, Stella (born 1971), and James Louis (born 1977). For that, he offers no apologies. "They say: 'Here's old family man Paulie, back with the sheep, what a yawn.' If I were really concerned with image I'd always be down in the clubs, buying them drinks and popping pills just to show them how hip I am. But it reaches a point where it just doesn't work; you can't live for all that. I'm trying not to bother with that stuff now."

John Lennon—Man in the Mirror

Toward the beginning of his solo career, John Lennon said of the Beatles' breakup: "People keep talking about it as if it's the end of the world. It's only a rock band. You have all the old records if you want to reminisce. The problem is that even the young people cannot accept change."

John himself seemed eager to burn all his bridges to the past. Just days after the Beatles were Officially Pronounced Dead by Paul McCartney, the Lennons traveled to California for four months of Dr. Arthur Janov's Primal Scream therapy. Cut off from the outside world, Janov's patients are encouraged to relive painful events from their early childhood on. This triggers the Primal Scream, with which neurotics may literally scream away their hangups. Lennon emerged from the experience feeling "reborn," as he put it in one of his new songs, *I was the Walrus, but now I'm John.*

His first post-Beatle LP was the direct result of Dr. Janov's intense form of psychotherapy. Nicknamed "the Primal Album," *John Lennon/Plastic Ono Band* exposed the bare wires of John's personal emotions more completely than any other record he has ever made. Songs such as "Mother"—in which he relives the pain caused by not having been wanted by his own parents—

build up to chilling primal screams. Other numbers reveal Lennon's bitter feelings toward school, drugs, straights, hippies, poverty, and fame. In the album's Big Statement, "God," John lists all the "myths" he once believed in but has now rejected: "magic," "Bible," "mantra," "Elvis," and finally, "Beatles." *I just believe in me*, he sings. *The dream is over.*

With *Plastic Ono Band*, John stripped his music down to the bare bones. On most songs his voice and guitar—or piano—are joined only by Ringo's drums and Klaus Voorman's bass. Each note and word sounds as if it were wrenched straight from the gut.

Plastic Ono Band was at once one of the most courageous and one of the most egotistical rock records ever. Courageous because—in a much deeper sense than the *Two Virgins* cover—it stripped John naked to the whole world; egotistical because he expected the world to view his nakedness as an important work of art.

He called the album his "Sgt. Lennon," and some critics still consider it the greatest of all the Beatles' solo records. But many people did not enjoy listening to John's "pain"—or to his dismissal of the Beatles as a faded dream. *Plastic Ono Band* sold far less well than Harrison's *All Things Must Pass*—or even *McCartney* and *Ram*.

To promote his album, John gave an extraordinary interview to *Rolling Stone*'s Jann Wenner. It was so long that it filled most of two issues and, eventually, a whole book called *Lennon Remembers*. As if he were still on his psychiatrist's couch, John unloaded a lifetime's worth of secrets. For the first time, an unsuspecting world learned the full extent of John's former involvement with drugs, his mixed feelings about many of the Beatles' accomplishments, and his sharp differences with Paul.

The Lennon-McCartney feud was soon to spill right into the words of the ex-Beatles' own songs. When Paul's *Ram* appeared, much of it made little sense to most listeners. John, however, thought numbers such as "Too Many People Preaching Practices"—with their lines about silly boys breaking their lucky

John and Yoko after their 1975
"retirement" (*Rex Features*)

breaks in two—were snide digs at himself.

Never one to beat around the bush, Lennon grabbed his poison pen and composed an open letter to McCartney. This was "How Do You Sleep?," a song on John's 1971 LP *Imagine*. With George Harrison adding some stinging guitar licks to show whose side *he* was on, Lennon attacked his rival for being nothing more than a "pretty face," who should have "learned something in all those years" but instead makes records that sound like Muzak. Those who had thought Paul McCartney was dead, John sang, were right after all. To add insult to injury, *Imagine* was even packaged with a photo of Lennon fondling a pig in an obvious takeoff of Paul's *Ram* LP cover.

The rest of *Imagine*, however, turned out to be surprisingly gentle and tuneful. "We told John he had to go more commercial if he wanted a big smash," admitted one of Allen Klein's assistants. *Imagine* was indeed an enormous smash, largely on the strength of the title song—whose vision of a world without countries, greed, or hunger seemed more like that of the 1969 peace crusader than the 1970 primal screamer.

The Lennons' next move was to New York City, with which John fell passionately in love. "Two thousand years ago," he said, "we'd all want to live in Rome. This is Rome now." The couple took up residence in a Greenwich Village brownstone, before finally settling into twenty-eight rooms of the exclusive, castle-like Dakota building overlooking Central Park.

John soon fell in with a crowd of New York radicals and Yippies. As unable as ever to do anything halfway, Lennon became totally absorbed by the world of revolutionary politics. And, as always, John's latest obsession was strongly reflected in his next album.

The cover of 1972's *Sometime in New York City* was designed as a parody of *The New York Times*, with the titles and words of the new songs printed in the style of newspaper headlines and articles. Alas, the Lennons' musical "statements" about Northern Ireland, Women's Liberation, and the Attica State Prison riots could not have been more witless and unimaginative. All the most tired and embarrassing slogans of the sixties' radical movement were now being parroted by the Beatle who used to have such a marvelous way with words.

Some Time in New York City failed to rise any higher than number forty-eight on the U.S. album charts—only nine months after *Imagine* had hit Number One. *Rolling Stone*, which shared John's left-wing political views, said Lennon had committed "artistic suicide" with his obnoxious and simple-minded new album. Like Paul before him, John was widely dismissed as a washed-out has-been.

The Lennons certainly had their share of problems at the time. First, Yoko's former husband Tony Cox kidnapped their daughter Kyoko. The Lennons' unsuccessful attempt to regain custody of Yoko's child dragged them on a wild-goose chase involving private detectives and complicated lawsuits.

Then the Nixon Administration began to see Lennon's political views as a serious threat. In John's four-year-old marijuana arrest, Attorney General Mitchell found the perfect excuse for ordering the ex-Beatle thrown out of the country. John challenged the government in court, while thousands of his fans busied themselves circulating petitions on Lennon's behalf. The case dragged on for three years, during which period John was forced to stay in the United States for fear that if he left he would never be allowed back in.

In 1973, Lennon tried to make a comeback with an album called *Mind Games*. In contrast to his deadly serious earlier records, *Mind Games* was filled with playful music and zany puns. Above all, it showed John trying to think positively for a change. "Yes is the answer," went one of his refrains. Once again, he was telling listeners to "chant the mantra" and "raise the spirits of peace and love." It was almost as if he'd never launched his solo career with the words, *I don't believe in magic . . . don't believe in mantra.* But John Lennon had never been famous for being consistent. "I'm back to believing everything until it's disproved," he explained.

Still, *Mind Games* lacked the cutting edge of John's best work.

For the first time in his career, he was recycling his old ideas. Also—like all the other ex-Beatles and almost everyone else in the mid-seventies—he was letting technical perfection squeeze the life out of his rock 'n' roll. All those 64-track machines and ultraprofessional session musicians were exactly what would cause the late seventies punk rock/New Wave rebellion. After *Some Time in New York City*, however, *Mind Games* did serve to clear the air and put John back on the music world's map.

Up to their old tricks again, the Lennons announced their invention of an imaginary country. "Nutopia," they declared, "has no land, no boundaries, no passports, only people. As two ambassadors of Nutopia, we ask for recognition in the United Nations of our country." The last song on side one of *Mind Games* was listed as "The Nutopian National Anthem"—but because it consisted merely of a few seconds of silence, most listeners remained unaware of its existence.

Nineteen seventy-four was probably the unhappiest year of John's adult life. After a falling-out with Yoko Ono, he set up shop in Los Angeles in the company of his Chinese secretary, May Pang. Lennon began working with Phil Spector on an album of fifties "oldies"—but halfway through the project, the producer disappeared with the tapes. John's unsuccessful attempt to track down the mysterious Spector kept him in California for six months.

Increasingly John took to drowning his troubles in booze. He turned up in the news as a wretched drunk. In one incident, he was charged with striking a waitress who tried to make him leave a nightclub after Lennon disrupted a Smothers Brothers performance.

John returned to New York during the summer of 1974. In a mere two weeks, he wrote and recorded a brand-new album. Much of it dealt with the painful and confused emotions that Lennon had experienced during what he called his "Sindbad's voyage" to California. Because these songs described the "walls" with which he protected himself from the outside world, and the "bridges" he nonetheless tried to build to his fellow human beings, John called the LP *Walls and Bridges.*

This album successfully combined the playful humor of *Mind Games,* the tunefulness and commercial sense of *Imagine,* and the raw honesty of *Plastic Ono Band.* There was even another musical poison-pen letter to "an old friend of mine" who has spread his "smell like an alley cat." The target of "Steel and Glass" appeared to be Allen Klein, with whom John, George, and Ringo were now exchanging multimillion dollar lawsuits.

Walls and Bridges also contained the upbeat single that best summed up Lennon's current attitude toward life: "Whatever Gets You Thru the Night, 'Salright, 'Salright." The ex-Beatle agreed to appear in concert with Elton John if "Whatever Gets You Thru the Night" hit Number One—"never thinking in a million years that it would." When it did anyway, Lennon gamely turned up onstage at Madison Square Garden to sing his new hit, along with "Lucy in the Sky with Diamonds" and a song "by an old fiancée of mine called Paul"—"I Saw Her Standing There." In this way, John let the world know that there were no more hard feelings between him and his ex-partner.

Soon after completing the highly successful *Walls and Bridges,* John finally managed to recover his California tapes and complete the *Rock 'n' Roll* oldies album without Phil Spector. Released in February 1975, *Rock 'n' Roll* brilliantly recaptured the spirit that, nearly twenty years earlier, had first set the magical mystery tour in motion. Yet it remains—as of this writing—the last that the music world has heard from John Lennon.

Patching things up with Yoko, John quietly moved back into his rooms at the Dakota. "The separation," he told reporters, "didn't work out." On October 7, Lennon's lengthy court battle with the government finally ended when the United States granted John his Green Card, allowing him to stay as long as he wished. Two days later—on the former Beatle's own thirty-fifth birthday—Yoko gave birth to the couple's first son, Sean Ono Lennon. Said John: "I feel higher than the Empire State Building."

After this, a veil of mystery seemed to fall over the Lennons' lives. Occasionally they turned up at glittering events, such as President Jimmy Carter's inaugural party. John and Yoko bought a cow farm in upstate New York and took several trips to Japan. On one of these, John was finally cornered into making a statement for the press: "We've basically decided, without a great decision, to be with our baby as much as we can until we feel we can take time off to indulge ourselves in creating things outside the family."

The Lennons' life style was beginning to resemble that of the McCartneys a few years earlier—which John had seemed so scornful of at the time. The difference, however, was that family and farm did not inspire Lennon to write songs about his cozy existence. "I have a new life," he said. "A new home—here in New York. I am happy here. I have made my contribution to society. I have no plans to work again."

But as the years crept by without any new Lennon music, the demand for John's "return" began to resemble the clamor for a Beatles' reunion. Lennon, however, has always used his solo music as a mirror, with which to capture his private angels and demons. Because John has such depth as an artist and as a man, millions of listeners were also able to discover part of themselves in his songs. But this highly personal approach is hardly suited to cranking out records just for the sake of having something in the marketplace—as other ex-Beatles have been accused of doing. During the second half of the seventies, John apparently felt he had nothing special to say.

The Lennons were, however, moved to offer a few typically mysterious clues on May 27, 1979. In a full-page ad in *The New York Times*, they announced that they had undergone a "Spring Cleaning of our minds.

"The things we have tried to achieve in the past by flashing a V sign, we try now through wishing," John and Yoko wrote. "Wishing is more effective than waving flags. It works. It's like magic. Magic is simple. Try it sometime.

"The house is getting very comfortable now. Sean is beautiful. The plants are growing. The cats are purring. The town is shin-

ing, sun, rain, or snow. We are thankful every day for the plenti-
fulness of our life.

"Many people are sending us vibes every day in letters, tele-
grams, taps on the gate, or just flowers and nice thoughts. We
thank them all and appreciate them for respecting our quiet
space, which we need.

"Our silence is a silence of love and not of indifference. We
are writing in the sky instead of on paper—that's our song. Lift
up your eyes and look up in the sky. There's our message."

George Harrison—The Dark Horse

Unlike Paul or John, George Harrison would probably not have
had the nerve to deal the greatest band on earth its official death
blow. But once his stronger co-Beatles had done the dirty work,
it was George who seemed—at first—to benefit most from the
split.

His first "real" solo album was nearly six months in the making. Because George had so many songs left over from the days
when the others allowed him only two per album, *All Things
Must Pass* turned out to be a *triple* record set. Like *John Lennon /
Plastic Ono Band*—also released just before Christmas 1970—
Harrison's album was good enough to make many fans forget the
absence of the usual Beatles Yuletide offering. But, while John's
unpolished songs were bitter attacks on everything Lennon had
once believed in—including "mantra," "Krishna" and "God"—
George's grand productions offered quite the opposite message.
Most of his songs amounted to religious sermons, or hymns of
praise to his Lord.

Both John's and George's records were actually coproduced by
the same man, Phil Spector. But, unlike Lennon, Harrison allowed Spector to live up to his reputation for creating great
"walls of sound" with a full rock 'n' roll orchestra. *All Things
Must Pass* featured a "cast of thousands"—including Ringo, Eric

Clapton, Badfinger and "the George O'Hara-Smith Singers." These last turned out to be the voices of Harrison himself, painstakingly overdubbed dozens of times to give the effect of a large choir. *Rolling Stone's* reviewer described the result as "the music of mountain tops and vast horizons."

All Things Must Pass also contained a few less-towering productions that reflected the influence of Bob Dylan—with whom George, of all the Beatles, had grown closest. These included a pair of Dylan originals, and "Apple Scruffs"—George's tribute to the girls who continued to spend much of their lives on the steps outside whichever building a Beatle happened to be in at the time. Harrison's friend Al Aronowitz reported: "Outside the studio door, whether it rained or not, there was always a handful of Apple Scruffs, one of them a girl all the way from Texas. Sometimes George would record from 7 P.M. to 7 A.M. and there they would be, waiting through the night for a sign of recognition on his way out."

All Things Must Pass came as a delightful surprise to fans used to George's role as "the invisible Beatle." Its popularity was such that it outsold all three other Beatles' recent solo albums put together. But then "My Sweet Lord"—the Number One single off *All Things Must Pass*—got George into trouble. He was sued— and in 1976 found guilty—for having pinched the tune from the Chiffons' decade-old hit "He's So Fine." George's response was to write a number sarcastically describing the case, called "This Song."

Harrison, however, is also the most generous of the Beatles, the only one to have set aside many of his royalties for charity. This admirable side of his character came to the world's attention in 1971, when millions were left homeless by the India-Pakistan war over Bangladesh.

At the suggestion of Ravi Shankar—whose family had originated in Bangladesh—George decided to help the refugees with a pair of benefit concerts at New York's Madison Square Garden. For the August 1 shows, Harrison assembled a full-scale *All Things Must Pass* rock 'n' roll orchestra, including Ringo Starr.

George Harrison at his charity "Concert for Bangla Desh"—which featured a surprise appearance by Bob Dylan (*Keystone Press Agency*)

George even talked his friend Bob Dylan—who had not given an American concert in over five years—into making a surprise appearance.

The shows were a stunning success on every level. Together with the film and three-record live album that were made of the event, the concerts raised millions of dollars for the refugees. According to *Rolling Stone*: "The Bangla Desh benefit, in the magnificence of its music and the selflessness of its motives, was proof that the art and spirit [of the counterculture] are still alive."

Both John and Paul turned down invitations to appear. Instead, they kept themselves busy saying nasty things about one another in public, and writing dreadful albums like *Sometime in New York City* and *Wild Life*. At the time, George seemed like the only real hero to have survived the wreckage of the Beatles.

All this goodwill helped make his 1973 release, *Living in the Material World*, the fastest-selling Beatle solo album yet. Though George produced it without Phil Spector, the new record featured grand arrangements and echoey, breathy voices in the best *All Things Must Pass* style. On most of the songs, Harrison tried to put across his mystical beliefs with slow, dreamlike music that sent some listeners into a happy trance and others straight to sleep. Like the next few Harrison albums, *Living in the Material World* was dedicated to Krishna, and packaged with pictures showing scenes from the Hindu holy scriptures. Some critics began to find this as annoying in its way as the family snapshots with which Paul decorated *his* record covers.

The critics may have had a point there. Without the other Beatles, George—like John and Paul—was perhaps getting too wrapped up in his particular "trip" for his own good. Lennon insisted that "it's far better music now, because by the time the Beatles were at our peak we were cutting each other down to size." But it was exactly that "cutting each other down to size" that, in many people's opinion, made *the Beatles* so much better.

John, Paul, George, and Ringo had each brought different strengths and talents to the group, while canceling out one another's weaknesses. John would, for instance, have laughed Paul right out of the studio had McCartney tried to introduce one of his sillier love songs—let alone "Mary Had a Little Lamb"—into a Beatles session. Paul would never have put up with John's more tiresome political slogans. And both would surely have brought George down to earth in a jiffy, had he threatened to get too pompous and holy. So, while it's true that great records such as *All Things Must Pass* and *Plastic Ono Band* could never have been made within the format of the Beatles, individual self-expression often became an excuse for self-indulgence.

At any rate, the warm welcome with which George's solo career had been received by the rock press was now starting to wear thin—though *Living in the Material World*'s exquisite music saved the day. But just one wrong move by George would give the critics their signal to shoot yet a third Beatle off his pedestal.

In late 1974, Harrison gave them all the ammunition they required. With the positive response to the Bangladesh benefits still fresh in his mind, George decided to go on the road again. Instead of testing the waters, Wings-style, in out-of-the-way European towns, George felt self-confident enough to plunge into a full-scale American tour—the first by an ex-Beatle.

He also wanted a new album in the shops, in time for the tour and the Christmas sales rush. But a tight schedule prevented George from giving the record the painstaking attention lavished on his earlier LPs. Due to overwork, he even lost his voice during the recording sessions. Harrison insisted on putting out *Dark Horse*—known to fans as *Dark Hoarse*—anyway.

The shows, which costarred Ravi Shankar, were as poorly received as the album. At times, George seemed barely able to croak out the words to his songs—which included very few made famous by the Beatles. And even these were almost unrecognizable; the very title of "While My Guitar Gently Weeps," for example, had been changed to "While My Guitar Gently *Smiles*." Beatlemaniacs did not exactly leap with delight.

Much to George's annoyance, his fans tended to become downright unruly when Ravi Shankar and his Indian orchestra took the stage. During one concert Harrison snapped, pointing at his own electric guitar: "I'd die for Indian music, but not for this."

The tour's exhausting pace—fifty concerts in twenty-seven cities over the course of six weeks—did little to improve George's voice or temper. Audiences were chewed out for smoking "dirty reefers" and drinking booze. "You won't find Lord Krishna in a bottle," lectured the ex-Beatle, sounding more like a stern preacher than a fun-loving rock star.

Still, many fans agreed with George that the music was far better than the reviews would have it. One such admirer was Jack Ford, at whose invitation Harrison dropped by the White House for a chat with the President. George gave Gerald Ford a Krishna button in exchange for one reading W.I.N. (Whip Inflation Now).

By late 1974, George's marriage—like those of John and Ringo—was also on the rocks. Patti Harrison had run off with her husband's best friend, Eric Clapton. Harrison made the news public during his tour's first press conference, when a reporter from "the women's pages" asked what he thought of his wife's cooking.

"I don't have a wife anymore," said George. "I learned to cook myself. I cook vegetarian Indian food, that's why I'm so pale and thin." He added that he was "very happy about" Patti's relationship with Clapton.

"Seriously?" gasped the lady reporter. "How can you be happy about it?"

"Because he's great. I'd rather have her with him than with some dope."

George had already found himself a beautiful new Mexican girl friend named Olivia Arras. The couple finally got married on August 31, 1978, a month after Olivia gave birth to George's first child, a boy named Dhani.

When Patti married Eric Clapton the following spring, Harrison, McCartney, and Starr all attended the wedding. At a private party afterward, the three ex-Beatles actually performed a few songs together for the other guests.

Both on record and in real life, George seems to have mellowed greatly since that 1974 tour—though his sour mood did spill over into 1975's *Extra Texture* LP. When the Beatles' contract with Capitol and EMI ran out in 1976, George was free to record for his own company, Dark Horse Records. Nineteen seventy-six's *Thirty-three and a Third* and 1979's *George Harrison* were as inspired, positive, and carefully crafted as *All Things Must Pass.* But the arrangements were far simpler, and the words much less preachy. Said George: "If you push 'My Sweet Lord' down people's throats too much, they jump back and try to bite you. That message has become a bit more subtle. 'Your Love Is Forever' is really saying the same old story. It's 'My Sweet Lord,' just done in a way which is less offensive to people—maybe through me getting older."

Harrison's passions in life now are racing cars and gardening. He is also a great friend and admirer of the British comedy group Monty Python. George has often been criticized in the past for seeming to lack a sense of humor about either religion or his own career. But the fact that he financed the Monty Python film *Life of Brian*—and actually appeared in Python member Eric Idle's TV special *The Rutles*—should put an end to such talk. *Life of Brian* is a highly disrespectful religious satire, and *The Rutles* a brilliantly detailed parody of everything you've been reading about in this very book.

For George Harrison, being a star has always come second to being a musician. Unlike Paul, he has never particularly enjoyed touring, giving interviews, and everything else that goes with staying in the public eye. George's own peace of mind is now more important to him than remaining in the headlines and at the top of the charts. "*We* sold more records than anybody," he says. "And as individuals, we've sold a few as well. We'll never individually be as big as the Beatles, and I'm glad, 'cause that was enough. We've *had* that experience."

These days, says George, "I don't go out of me way to sell records. If people like it they can buy it. I'll do what I can do as honestly as I can, but I'm not gonna turn into a punk, or go disco.

I don't *like* disco, so what's the point?

"I could go out and become a superstar, if I checked meself out and practiced a bit. But I don't really wanna do that, being a kamikazi pop star, the tours and everything. I don't have to prove anything."

Ringo Starr—The Bit-Part Player

When the Beatles broke up, few expected much from the sad-eyed little drummer who had written but two of the two hundred-odd tunes in the Beatles songbook. So everyone was most pleasantly surprised when Ringo eventually did pop up with a few very good records.

He began his career as a solo recording artist in 1970 by living out two of his pet fantasies. The first of these proved to be a bit of a disaster. Casting himself as the sort of Frank Sinatra–style crooner his mother had always adored, Ringo recorded *Sentimental Journey*, an album of songs from the twenties, thirties, and forties. This was the last thing Beatlemaniacs wished to hear from their favorite drummer—especially as Ringo sang the moldy oldies rather badly.

Starr's next project was less out of character. While working with him on George's *All Things Must Pass*, country-music wizard Pete Drake agreed to help the Liverpool cowboy realize his dream of making a real country record in Nashville. For Starr's *Beaucoups of Blues* album, Drake selected, produced, and played on all the songs; all Ringo needed to do was fly to the country music capital for two days to add his unmistakable voice. The result was hardly a creative breakthrough for Ringo Starr—but at least it did not embarrass his fans the way *Sentimental Journey* had.

Ringo also kept up his acting career. In the years following the Beatles split, he would make cameo appearances in seven movies—usually in the company of fellow rock stars. These ranged from a grade-C Western called *Blindman* to Mae West's

Ringo Starr in his highly praised role as a fifties'
greaser in *That'll Be the Day*, 1973 (*Rex Features*)

Sextette. Ringo's best-received role was that of a fifties greaser in *That'll Be the Day.* In 1972, he even attempted to direct his own documentary, *Born to Boogie,* about England's latest rock-music sensation, T. Rex.

Ringo made yet another career for himself designing fancy, offbeat furniture with his friend Robin Cruikshank. The pair opened a shop—Ringo Or Robin—at Apple Records' London headquarters. For sale there were such Starr brainwaves as a coffee table made out of Rolls-Royce grilles. Elton John's manager bought one for $5,000.

During 1971 and 1972, Ringo's musical output was limited to a pair of singles, "It Don't Come Easy" and "Back Off Boogaloo." George Harrison produced and played guitar on both. To many people's amazement, these Richard Starkey compositions turned out to be solid, catchy rock 'n' roll songs—and enormous hits.

Hard-core Beatlemaniacs were particularly intrigued by the B side of "It Don't Come Easy." Called "Early 1970," it described Ringo's feelings about the other Beatles at the time of the breakup. Paul is pictured as being too busy with family and farm to bother playing with his long-time drummer. John is also busy with Yoko, yet happy to play with Ringo when he can spare the time. George, however, is "always in town playing for you with me." Starr closes the song with a wish: "When I go to town I want to see all three." As "Early 1970" showed, Ringo was always the Beatle most in favor of the group's eventual reunion.

He almost brought one about—and certainly "went to town"—when he got on with making a "real" Ringo Starr album in 1973. George, as usual, was there from the start, helping out with songs such as "Photograph"—the first of three big hit singles to be pulled off the *Ringo* LP.

Then John turned up with a humorous new song about what it was like to have been one of the Beatles—"the greatest show on earth, for what it was worth." Fittingly, three of the original stars of that show—Ringo, George, and John—joined forces in the studio to record Lennon's "I'm the Greatest." The only ingredient missing from this nostalgic reunion was Paul McCartney.

But not to be outdone by his rival ex-Beatles, Paul came round in the end with a fine new McCartney ballad written especially for *Ringo*. On his "Six O'Clock," McCartney can be heard singing and playing piano and synthesizer. Paul also wrote the string and flute parts.

The easy-going Ringo was the only ex-Beatle who could have persuaded the other three to forget their differences and appear on the same record again. (The fact that Allen Klein was now out of the picture helped, too.) Ringo also enlisted the aid of other big names, such as the Band and Marc Bolan of T. Rex. The album's producer was Richard Perry, whose track record included numerous hits by Barbra Streisand and Carly Simon.

But Ringo's simple voice and happy-go-lucky personality are never lost amidst the all-star lineup and slick production. Among such close and talented friends, all he had to do was act naturally—and the hits just kept right on coming. After *Ringo*'s "You're 16" and "Oh My My" followed "Photograph" to the top of the charts, John Lennon—whose own recent records had been selling far less well—shot off a telegram to his old drummer: CONGRATULATIONS. HOW DARE YOU? AND PLEASE WRITE ME A HIT SONG.

But Starr and Perry proved unable to repeat the magic *Ringo* formula. Without the enthusiastic participation of the right set of friends, Ringo's records tended to become painfully dull. Despite some contributions from assorted ex-Beatles and other superstars, 1974's *Goodnight Vienna* and 1976's *Rotogravure* did not exactly set the music world on its ear.

Ringo's personal life, however, continued to make news. With his marriage to Maureen on the rocks, Starr was photographed in the company of such glamorous dates as singer/actress Lindsey de Paul and photographer Nancy Andrews. Fleeing Britain's greedy taxman, he took up residence in Monte Carlo. During one of his stays there, Ringo drew headlines by shaving his head completely bald, Kojak-style. He also spent a lot of time in Los Angeles, partying with the stars.

When the Beatles' contract with EMI and Capitol ran out in

1976, Atlantic Records paid Ringo a great deal of money to sign with them. The ex-Beatle was teamed up with Atlantic's top producer, Arif Mardin, who had recently used the new disco beat to shake the Bee Gees' career out of the doldrums. Mardin planned to do the same for Ringo Starr.

But Ringo proved to be a very different sort of recording artist from the Bee Gees. The Brothers Gibb were the musical equivalent of chameleons, with a great knack for writing and singing in whatever style happened to be popular at the time. (They had made their original fortune in the late sixties by copying the Beatles' psychedelic sounds.) Ringo's frail talents, however, could hardly have been less well-suited to the mechanical disco beat.

Records such as *Ringo the Fourth* reduced the ex-Beatle to a faceless cog in a disco hit-factory. But in Ringo's case there were no hits, as all his old fans were completely turned off. The disco audience wasn't interested either.

Even after Atlantic Records dropped him, Ringo refused to give up. In 1978 he made a nondisco LP, *Bad Boy*, for Portrait Records, and starred in a TV special. Loosely based on Mark Twain's *The Prince and the Pauper*, this was a fantasy in which Ringo traded places with his nonmusical double. But the poor response to both show and album suggested that Ringo's days as a current force on the music scene were long over.

Still, who in 1970 would have expected him to accomplish as much as he has? Without the support of highly creative people who know and care about him enough to tailor their own talents to his needs, Ringo Starr can only remain what people loved him as all along: "One of history's most charming bit-part players."

Beatles 4-Ever

Around the middle of the 1970s, the Beatles passed into history. By this time, everything they had seemed to stand for had been pretty well absorbed by society at large. A boy who happened to wear his hair long, listen to rock music, or smoke marijuana could no longer necessarily be considered a rebel against his parents, teachers, or the government. Like the divisive Vietnam war and Richard Nixon's presidency, that "us" and "them" attitude separating the counterculture from the "straight" world was now a thing of the past. The teen-agers who had turned on, tuned in, and dropped out to the beat of the Beatles and Bob Dylan found themselves nearing their thirties, becoming less interested in protests against society's shortcomings than in a good job and a decent living in the material world.

People began to sense that the Beatles represented a time that was now behind them. Some of the solo albums were very enjoyable, and some less so; but nobody could claim that even *Band on the Run* or *Walls and Bridges* captured and shaped the mood of the times the way each Beatles record had. If, say, *Dark Horse* or *Ringo the Fourth* was disappointing, the fans no longer loved the Beatles any less for it, as they had when *Wild Life* and *Sometime in New York City* first came out. For the Beatles had become an airtight myth, locked forever into the 1960s.

Of course, there were some die-hard fans who liked to imagine that everything they fondly remembered about the sixties would return, as if by magic, should the fabulous foursome only come together again. But others had to agree with Yoko Ono when she compared the Beatles to the Golden Temple of an old Japanese fable. "A guy fell in love with it and burned it down. He couldn't stand the idea of its falling apart as it got older, and now the Golden Temple exists in perfect form forever. It became a myth. That's why the Beatles will stay a beautiful myth, because they ended before they deteriorated."

Only once the group had clearly become part of the past did the first signs of a "Beatle revival" begin to sweep the United States and much of the rest of the world. A lot of this was "sixties' nostalgia" on the part of those who had grown up with the Beatles. But the old-timers were gradually joined by millions of new Beatlemaniacs too young to remember the days when "I

Want to Hold Your Hand"—or even "Hey Jude"—had topped the hit parade. Some were drawn to the Beatle legend because they sensed there was nothing nearly so earthshaking going on in the rock music of the 1970s, and they wanted to catch up on what they thought they'd missed.

As more and more fans felt the desire to surround themselves with *things* that seemed to represent a piece of that legend, a new breed of Beatlemaniacs arose: the collector. Suddenly all those old Beatle gum cards, dolls, and lunch boxes were worth good money. Long-time fans who'd let their mothers throw out all that "junk" were pained to find such memorabilia on sale at flea markets and even in antique stores for ten times their original retail value. Pink plastic Beatle guitars from 1964 began changing hands for $75; the Flip Your Wig board game for $20; and a yellow submarine Corgi Toy for $25.

Similarly, hard-to-find Beatle records were going for a lot more than a song. Top collector's items included the original picture sleeves for the Beatles' singles; rip-off LPs put out in 1964 by companies that had since gone out of business; and, above all, the *Yesterday and Today* "butcher cover," which once drew $300 at an auction of Beatle memorabilia.

Fans and collectors even created their own special grapevine for getting in touch with each other. This took the form of "fanzines," amateur publications usually churned out on a mimeograph machine in some Beatlemaniac's basement. Often named after a song, such as *With a Little Help from My Friends* or *The Inner Light*, a Beatle fanzine would usually combine reprints of newsclippings, old and new, with collectors' ads and articles and artwork by ordinary fans.

Joe Pope, editor of the fine *Strawberry Fields Forever* fanzine, made Beatle fan history in Boston on July 26, 1974—with "Mystery Tour," the first full-scale Beatles convention. The festivities included a performance by a Beatle sound-alike group, screenings of such films as *The Beatles at Shea Stadium* and *Magical Mystery Tour*, and a giant flea market where collectors might buy, sell, and swap memorabilia.

This was followed two months later by a New York "Beatle-fest" organized by Mark Lapidos, which added such features as Beatles memorabilia auctions and look-alike/sound-alike contests, along with panel discussions involving people who had worked with or written about John, Paul, George, and Ringo. Both conventions have been repeated several times, and Mark Lapidos has taken his show to other cities across the United States. Many fans thought nothing of traveling hundreds of miles to take advantage of these opportunities to add to their collections and to meet and party with fellow Beatlemaniacs. Similar events have since been staged in England, Holland, and France.

The Beatle revival was sparked by the hard-core fans and collectors, but it was not long before record companies, publishers, and theater and film producers began to cash in on the trend. For the first time in years, slick Beatle magazines (usually far less knowledgeable and interesting than the fanzines) turned up on newsstands. Eventually there would even be an excellent Marvel Comics version of the Beatles' story.

Beatle plays and musicals opened in New York and London. They ranged from a fine dramatization of the Beatles' lives (*John, Paul, George, Ringo . . . and Bert*), to a flashy variety show vaguely based on their songs (*Sgt. Pepper's Lonely Hearts Club Band*), to an imitation Beatle concert coupling a sound-alike group with slides and films of the sixties (*Beatlemania*). This last was the most successful with the ticket-buying public and the least successful with the critics—who, like many long-time fans, found the show a cheap mockery of true Beatlemania as they remembered it. The Beatles themselves eventually sued *Beatlemania*'s producers for $60 million. Still, lots of younger fans who had missed out on the real thing evidently felt that an artificial Beatle concert was better than none at all.

But the use of the Beatles' name and music was in itself no guarantee of big profits. The films *I Wanna Hold Your Hand, All This and World War II*, and the Peter Frampton/Bee Gees *Sgt. Pepper's Lonely Hearts Club Band* were all box-office failures—in the last two cases, deservedly so.

Amidst all this, the pressure mounted for the real Beatles to forget their differences and "get back to where they once belonged." In 1974, a promoter named Bill Sargent offered them $15 million to play one concert. By 1976, he had upped his bid to $60 million. Sargent figured he could get his money back by having the show broadcast closed-circuit to concert halls around the world—where fans would be charged a small fortune to, in effect, watch the Beatles on TV.

Sargent eventually got the message that John, Paul, George, and Ringo would never cheat their fans in this way even if they did decide to play together again in public. He finally gave up, and instead tried—also unsuccessfully—to organize a fight-to-the-death between a man and a killer shark. George Harrison cracked: "My suggestion was that *he* fight the shark, and the winner could promote the Beatles' concert!"

Sid Bernstein, who had once brought the Beatles to Carnegie Hall and Shea Stadium, also attempted to persuade them to reunite for a "simulcast" concert. In a 1976 full-page ad in *The New York Times* and other papers, Bernstein outlined a plan that he claimed could earn the group over $200 million from ticket sales, movie rights, and a double live album. He suggested that they could then use this money for "feeding and educating the orphan children of the needy nations." Bernstein meant well; but the Beatles seemed to resent the tone of his offer. George said sarcastically: "It was cute the way the ad in *The Times* tried to put the responsibility for saving the world on our shoulders." In the autumn of 1979, however, Bernstein tried again; and even United Nations Secretary-General Kurt Waldheim was said to have asked the Beatles to do a reunion concert benefiting the Indochinese "boat people."

All the Beatles were wary of the unreal expectations people would have for such a concert. As John Lennon put it in 1969, before the Beatles had even officially split up: "Whatever happens we're going to get knocked. We have so much to live up to.

There's such a mystique about the Beatles that they'll be expecting God to perform—which we're not."

In any case, every Beatle except Ringo rated the chances for a reunion close to zero. Physically the four were scattered to almost as many corners of the world, and musically they had likewise branched out in different directions. It was hard to imagine them regrouping for love or money. And they certainly didn't need the money. Said George: "The Beatles are for the history books, like the year 1492."

In 1976 Capitol and EMI decided that the world was ready for new Beatle records. If John, Paul, George, and Ringo weren't about to join forces in the studios, then the companies would have to make do with selling old wine in new bottles.

In Britain, the Beatles' twenty-two singles were reissued in bright new picture sleeves—along with "Yesterday," which until then had only been a *Help!* album track there. All twenty-three songs hit the Top Hundred, and "Yesterday" and "Hey Jude" made the Top Ten. Over a million singles were sold within a month.

For the U.S. market, Capitol picked out "Got to Get You into My Life," a relatively unknown but very commercial song from *Revolver.* The single was pushed as though it were a brand-new Beatle recording, and quickly became a major hit. Like so much of the Beatles' music, it sounded amazingly fresh and up-to-date on the radio, ten years after it had been recorded.

Since a pair of Beatles "greatest hits" LP's, *1962–1966* and *1967–1970,* had already been out for three years, Capitol tried a different tactic for coming up with a "new" album. Twenty-eight of the Beatles' loudest and fastest numbers were collected on a double-LP titled *Rock 'n' Roll Music.* (The following year it would be the turn of the soft and slow *Love Songs.*)

There was a lot wrong with *Rock 'n' Roll Music,* and according to Ringo, all the Beatles hated it. "The cover was disgusting," he complained. "It made us look cheap and we never were cheap. All the Coca-Cola and cars with big fins was the fifties." But despite its shortcomings, *Rock 'n' Roll Music* sold over a million copies within weeks after its release. Not bad for an album containing songs that had already appeared on as many as seven singles and LPs.

Capitol's next album offered more of a treat to long-time fans. This was the first official Beatles live recording, *The Beatles at the Hollywood Bowl*. Taped in 1964 and 1965, it hadn't been released at the time because the boys considered the quality of the recording and performance below the standard of the studio versions. That is true, and quite excusable considering the Beatles' inability to even hear themselves play over the deafening screams of their fans. But it is precisely that audience response which makes *The Beatles at the Hollywood Bowl* so astonishing to hear fifteen years later. No performers before or since have been able to stir up such absolute hysteria.

The year 1977 also saw the release of the unofficial *Live at the Star Club, Hamburg, Germany, 1962*. This album contained recordings a friend in the nightclub audience had made with his cheap home tape recorder. Now $100,000—as much as the Beatles had poured into the *Sgt. Pepper* recording sessions—was spent on applying complicated electronic treatments to the Hamburg tapes, in the vain hope of turning them into a listenable product. The Beatles themselves sued unsuccessfully to keep it off the market. Even so, *Live at the Star Club* in a sense brought the incredible story revealed by their records full circle—back to the Beatles' rough, unglamorous beginnings, when nobody could possibly have imagined that these four scruffy boys from Liverpool would one day set the tone for an entire generation.

The Beatles may have passed into another era now, but they have also passed the test of time. Every phase popular music enters—be it disco or New Wave—brings new hit versions of old Beatles songs, recorded by a new generation of stars. The Beatles' own classic albums still sell better than most current releases.

In the years to come, the records and books, films and plays, will doubtless continue to appear, each attempting a new angle on the story of the greatest group in the history of popular music.

The boys from Liverpool may have grown up and apart, but their legend seems certain to outlive the four Beatles themselves—and the millions whose lives were touched by their music and their magic.

Bibliography

Aldridge, Alan, ed. *The Beatles' Illustrated Lyrics*. Delacorte Press, 1969. The Beatles' best lyrics, illustrated in an appropriately psychedelic style by such top 1960s artists as Milton Glaser, Peter Max, and Ronald Searle. Also included are relevant quotes from the Beatles themselves. A second volume appeared in 1971.

Braun, Michael. *Love Me Do*. Penguin, 1964. The only one of several early "quickie" paperbacks to offer a realistic and insightful picture of the Beatles during their first year at the top.

Carr, Roy and Tyler, Tony. *The Beatles: An Illustrated Record*. 2d rev. ed. Harmony, 1978. A chronological review of every Beatle and ex-Beatle record by two critics from the London *New Musical Express;* lavishly illustrated.

Castleman, Harry and Podrazik, Wally. *All Together Now*. Pierian Press, 1976. (paperback edition, Ballantine, 1977). An extensive and detailed discography listing virtually every record any of the Beatles ever had anything to do with. Pierian Press issued a second volume, *The Beatles Again*, in 1977.

Davies, Hunter. *The Beatles*. 2d rev. ed. McGraw-Hill, 1978. The only authorized biography of the Beatles, and especially strong on their Liverpool backgrounds.

Davis, Edward E., ed. *The Beatles Book*. Cowles, 1968. A collection of essays written about the Beatles in the mid-sixties by composer Ned Rorem, Conservative columnist William F. Buckley, LSD advocate Timothy Leary, and eleven others.

di Franco, Philip, ed. *The Beatles: A Hard Day's Night.* Chelsea House, 1977. (paperback edition, Penguin, 1978). The complete screenplay of the Beatles' first and best film, together with an extended interview with director Richard Lester, and hundreds of stills from the movie.

McCabe, Peter and Schonfeld, Robert D. *Apple to the Core: The Unmaking of the Beatles.* Pocket Books, 1972. The definitive account of the business intrigues behind the Beatles' break-up.

Miles, Barry, ed. *Mersey Beat: The Beginnings of the Beatles.* Omnibus Press, 1978. (paperback edition, music sales, 1978). Replica pages from *Mersey Beat*, an early 1960s' Liverpool pop music newspaper, which document the Beatles' rise from a local cult to international stardom.

Schaffner, Nicholas. *The Beatles Forever.* Cameron House/Stackpole Books, 1977. (rev. paperback edition, McGraw-Hill, 1978). A detailed chronicle of the Beatles phenomenon, with hundreds of illustrations of memorabilia and record covers from all over the world.

Wenner, Jann. *Lennon Remembers.* Straight Arrow, 1971. (paperback edition, Popular Library, n.d.). The longest and most revealing interview ever given by a Beatle.

Many of the above books provided source material for the present volume. All are recommended for further reading. Information and short quotes were also gleaned from *The Beatles Monthly Book* and such music periodicals as *Rolling Stone, Billboard, New Musical Express,* and *Melody Maker;* from the autobiographies of Brian Epstein (*A Cellarful of Noise,* Doubleday, 1964) and Ravi Shankar (*My Music, My Life,* Simon and Schuster, 1968); and from interviews conducted with members of the Beatles and their entourage by David Wigg, Barry Miles, Tony Palmer, Ray Conolly, and Maureen Grant. Further assistance in compiling this book was kindly provided by Linda Patrick, Sue Weiner, and Mary Gimbel.

Index